LIFE SKILLS FOR TEENAGE GIRLS BIBLE [5 IN 1]

The Complete Handbook for Building a Strong Foundation for the Future

HANNAH HEWITT

THIS COLLECTION INCLUDES THE FOLLOWING BOOKS:

BEYOND THE BODY: The Art of Self-Acceptance: Embrace your True Self

YOUR CHANGING BODY: Empowering your Mind and Body: Navigating Puberty and Mental Health

THE WORLD AROUND YOU: Your Way to an Independent Life: Navigating Relationships and Society

THE SOCIAL FACTOR Being: Your Authentic Self: Embracing the Power of Your Identity and Community

YOUR PERSONAL WORKBOOK: Speak Your Truth: Discovering Your Voice and Unlocking Your Potential

© **Copyright - All rights reserved.**

The content contained within this book may not be reproduced, duplicated, or transmitted without direct written permission from the author or the publisher.

Under no circumstances will any blame or legal responsibility be held against the publisher, or author, for any damages, reparation, or monetary loss due to the information contained within this book, either directly or indirectly.

Legal Notice:

This book is copyright protected. It is only for personal use. You cannot amend, distribute, sell, use, quote, or paraphrase any part, or the content within this book, without the consent of the author or publisher.

Disclaimer Notice:

Please note the information contained within this document is for educational and entertainment purposes only. All effort has been executed to present accurate, up to date, reliable and complete information. No warranties of any kind are declared or implied. Readers acknowledge that the author is not engaging in the rendering of legal, financial, medical, or professional advice. The content within this book has been derived from various sources. Please consult a licensed professional before attempting any techniques outlined in this book.

By reading this document, the reader agrees that under no circumstances is the author responsible for any losses, direct or indirect, that are incurred as a result of the use of the information contained within this document, including, but not limited to, errors, omissions, or inaccuracies.

Table of Contents

INTRODUCTION
DISCOVER YOUR INNER SUPER STAR

BOOK 1 – BEYOND THE BODY
The Art of Self-Acceptance: Embrace your True Self

INTRODUCTION _____ 5
CHAPTER 1 – MIRROR, MIRROR ON THE WALL_____ 7
   Chrissy's Quest for Confidence: Crush your Insecurities _____ 7
   Why is my mirror not my friend? Discovering True Beauty _____ 8
   Navigating the Outside world: Your Inner Strength _____ 10
   Something to Ponder: The Power of Self-Love and Acceptance ____ 10
   Reality bites: Confronting your Insecurities and Owning your Beauty _ 11
   Let's get down to business: Mastering your Appearance and Attitude _ 12
   Taking the reins into your own hands: Empowerment and Self Discovery _____ 13

CHAPTER 2 - SKINTASTIC _____ 16
   Abby's Battle with Skin Woes: Secrets to Radiant Skin and Hair ____ 16
   Uncovering your Skin's Potential: Understanding Changes in Skin ___ 17
   The Art of Make up: Enhancing your Natural Beauty _____ 20
   Maximising the Power of your Skin: General Skin Care _____ 21

CHAPTER 3 - HAIR MATTERS _____ 23
   Marina's impulsive decision: Hair, Hair Everywhere! _____ 23
   A bit of theory: Mastering the Art of Hair Care _____ 24
   Hair Care Regimen: Unlocking your Hair's Potential _____ 25
   Something to remember: Tips for Gorgeous and Healthy Hair _____ 27

BOOK 2 – YOUR CHANGING BODY
Empowering your Mind and Body: Navigating Puberty and Mental Health

INTRODUCTION _____ 31

CHAPTER 1 - PHASES OF CHANGE _____ 33

Aunty Flo comes a visiting- Understanding your Body's Changes ____ 33

Signs of Puberty: Taking Control of your Body and Mind _____ 34

Menstruation: What Actually is it? _____ 34

How can you handle your periods like a pro? _____ 35

PMS and PMDD: How to Spot and Address Them _____ 36

Hair growth _____ 39

Increase in Breast size _____ 40

Your daily care routine: Mastering the Art of Self Care _____ 42

Nail Care: Tips and Tricks for GorgeousNails _____ 42

CHAPTER 2 - MIND MATTERS _____ 45

Elsa's Attitude: Mastering your Mental Health _____ 45

Understanding Mental Health and its Challenges: Strengthening your Mind _____ 46

Spotting Mental Health Issues and Taking Control of your Life _____ 48

Diving in _____ 48

How to Address Mental Health Issues Effectively and Live your Best Life _____ 48

CHAPTER 3 - VIVA LA BODY _____ 53

Why in the shopping aisle? Fuelling your Mind and Body with Healthy Habits _____ 53

Eating Healthy: Tiny Steps to a Better Lifestyle: Change Your Eating Habits and Transform Your Life! _____ 54

Physical Activity for a Healthy Body: Working out _____ 56

A Few Things to Remember: Tips and Tricks for a Healthier You _____ 57

Shopping Right: Building a Healthy and Sustainable Lifestyle through Mindful Consumerism _____ 58

BOOK 3 – THE WORLD AROUND YOU
Your way to an Independent Life: Navigating Relationships and Society

INTRODUCTION _____ 65
CHAPTER 1 - PEER PRESSURE _____ 67

Abby and Brielle: Navigating Peer Pressure like a Pro _____ 67

What is Peer Pressure? Understanding its Forms and Effects _____ 69

How to Nip Peer Pressure in the Bud and Stay True to Yourself _____ 71

Bullying: Standing up to your Bullies and Building Resilience _____ 73

Making friends: Tips and Tricks for Meeting New People and Building Strong Relationships _____ 74

CHAPTER 2 – MIND YOUR BUSINESS _____ 78

A mom was a child too...once upon a time: Achieving Independence _ 78

Societal Pressure: Overcoming the Fear of Fitting In _____ 79

Seeking Validation: Learning to Love Yourself and Put Yourself First _ 81

People Pleasing: Tips for Breaking the Cycle and Living your Best Life 82

The Independent Teenager _____ 84

Practising Independence _____ 86

Moving Out: Signs you Need to Move out of your Parent's Home and Build your Own Life _____ 87

BOOK 4 – THE SOCIAL FACTOR
Your Authentic Self: Embracing the Power of Identity and Community

INTRODUCTION _____ **96**

CHAPTER 1 – THE SOCIAL INFLUENCE FACTOR _____ **98**

    The Façade: Shedding the Masks and Finding your True Identity ____ 98

    False Positivity: Embracing Your True Feelings and Emotions _____ 99

    Influence: Navigating the Social World and Finding Your Voice _____ 102

    How to Take Back Control and Be Your Most Authentic Self _____ 103

CHAPTER 2 – FROM SCROLLS TO TROLLS _____ **106**

    A Word to the Wise: Navigating the World of Social Media _____ 106

    Using Social Media in the Right Way: Tips and Tricks for Building Your Online Presence and Making a Positive Impact _____ 110

BOOK 5 – YOUR PERSONAL WORKBOOK

Speak your truth: Discovering your Voice and Unlocking your Potential

INTRODUCTION _____ **114**

JOURNAL PROMPTS UNLEASHING THE POWER OF YOUR THOUGHTS AND FEELINGS _____ **115**

    Why is journaling so important? Understanding the Benefits and Power of Self-Reflection _____ 115

A NOTE FROM THE AUTHOR EMBRACE YOUR INNER SUPERSTAR AND LIVE YOUR BEST LIFE! _____ **140**

INTRODUCTION
DISCOVER YOUR INNER
SUPER STAR

Do you feel uncomfortable in your body?
Do you wish people wouldn't look at you the way they do?
Do you wish puberty wasn't such an awkward phase?

If you are nodding fervently right about now, then this book is exactly what you need.

Body image is a concept that isn't new. Believe me I've been there too. After all, I was a teenager once....oh those days filled with a myriad challenges and so many setbacks, but enough about me. Let's talk about you, yes YOU.

As a mother of three teenagers, I have seen it all. I have been introduced to every zit, every kind of friend, bully and the cocktail of emotions that are a staple of every teenager. But beyond seeing it all, I understand it all and I empathise with you.

This phase is never easy. It never was and no teenager ever sailed through the teen years saying.....'Oh that was a breeze'. But if you learn how to navigate through the challenges that come your way and know what to expect, then you are in a better position than so many others out there. In the midst of the sea that you seem to be surrounded by, any help is welcome right?

This book covers everything you need to know about your body by segmenting it into easy-to-read books.

Book 1: BEYOND THE BODY: The Art of Self-Acceptance: Embrace your True Self

In this book you will not only understand how to love and accept your physical self but also understand the changes that you will experience in your skin, hair, and body.

Book 2: YOUR CHANGING BODY: Empowering your Mind and Body: Navigating Puberty and Mental Health

This book uncovers the facts about puberty and how the hormonal changes in your body will affect you. It divulges the truth about mental health and teaches you to make better lifestyle decisions by eating right, and also including a fitness routine into your life.

Book 3: THE WORLD AROUND YOU: Your Way to an Independent Life: Navigating Relationships and Society

This book reveals the highs and lows of peer pressure and bullying. It shows you how to handle your family, friends, and society with panache and become independent. It also teaches you how to make the right friends and overcome people pleasing.

BOOK 4 – THE SOCIAL FACTOR Being: Your Authentic Self: Embracing the Power of Your Identity and Community

This book helps you embrace your authenticity by taking charge of your life and finding your voice. It discloses the pros and cons of social media and how to harness its power to your benefit.

BOOK 5: YOUR PERSONAL WORKBOOK: Speak Your Truth: Discovering Your Voice and Unlocking Your Potential

This fun book helps you know exactly how to journal and the benefits that you can gain from it. It gives you a safe space to jot down your notes in.

Honestly, I wish someone had given me this book when I was a teenager. I am not simply saying this because I wrote it. As you read on, you'll see what I mean.

My sincere wish for you is to have a more fulfilling life and to focus on the priorities, as well as the people that really matter in your life, rather than feel bogged down by your emotions and negative thought patterns. I hope that this book and the journal prompts at the end of each chapter help you face your own feelings and emotions with courage, so you can take charge of your life.

If you feel like a fish out of water, it is about time you learn to overcome the struggles mentioned in this book, that seem all too familiar.

Imagine a life where you wake up every morning embracing puberty. You accept it for what it is and not for what it could be. You get out of your own head and live in the real world instead. You identify the bullies, make the right friends who make you feel good, consume the appropriate content, and take care of your physical and mental health. You learn to do things for yourself and become independent. Teenage life no longer sucks.

This book, entirely backed by research and personal experience, teaches you what it means to be a 'live and let live' kind of teenager and make sense of your world.

As I mentioned above, your personal workbook included at the end covers all the questions I ask you to consider while reading the book. You can choose to respond to them at the end of each chapter or altogether once you finish reading the entire book. The choice is yours. There is also a section where you can make notes you like from each chapter, for easy recall. To help you with it, the end of each chapter gives you a summary of what was covered as well.

Read on to see exactly what I mean.....see you inside.

BOOK 1

BEYOND THE BODY

The Art of Self-Acceptance: Embrace your True Self

INTRODUCTION

As the title suggests, this book teaches you how to look beyond the realm of your physical appearance. You are not only your physical body alone. Your body changes, ages, fades, and withers over time. It's your brains, skills and personality that persist and live on. Yet we spend hours and hours obsessing over our bodies, comparing it to other people, hating our reflection and taking things a bit too personally. Looks fade but your personality is here to stay. Of course you can tweak that too, if you wish, with continued effort. But your physical appearance has a lot more to do with genetics than you might care to know about. Which means to show that there is not much that you can do by way of changing your looks other than taking extreme measures and that is certainly not going to be encouraged within the pages of this book. No missy! So, what choice do you have, you ask? Nothing beyond accepting yourself – looks and all. I know that might feel like a bitter pill to swallow but it is what it is.

This book drops some truth bombs straight off the bat. I believe that there is no use sugar coating stuff, is there? It's better that you know them, address them, and move on, rather than live a life filled with doubts and uncertainties or worse, look back with a mountain of regrets. **It's time to stop making excuses and start living life.**

Whether it's your mirror or your selfie camera or an actual human that is judging you and causing you to think differently about yourself, there is a way out of being a slave to your devices and the people around you. Whether you are battling with the changes in the look, texture and feel of your skin or the appearance of new hair on your body, you will learn what each of them mean and how you can address them. This phase is not a cake walk. There is so much going on. Gone are the days of silky-smooth baby skin and shiny hair. But all change is not bad and this one certainly isn't, although you feel like you are way out of your depth at first.

This book will show you how to change your outlook so that you look at yourself differently. Why should boys have all the fun? Let's own our bodies and everything that it comes with.

CHAPTER 1 – MIRROR, MIRROR ON THE WALL

"Dear you, make peace with the mirror and watch your reflection change"

In this chapter we will cover:

- Why looking in the mirror causes you distress.
- How to change the negative thought patterns that plague you, and make peace with yourself.

Chrissy's Quest for Confidence: Crush your Insecurities

My youngest daughter's name is Christina, we lovingly call her Chrissy. Her siblings call her Chris to annoy her. She is named after my grandmother. You will read several stories about my girls throughout the pages of these books but don't worry, they have all been pre-approved by them. They were the first ones to read the completed manuscript after all. Their hope is that you benefit from their learnings with their own personal struggles. I may also reference other teenagers and their stories in chapters to follow. However, their names have been changed to protect their identity, but it will still help you understand that there are others just like you out there. Basically, YOU ARE NOT ALONE!

I was walking by Christina's room one Saturday morning when she had just turned thirteen. She shares her room with my middle daughter Patricia (Patty). My eldest Abby has her own room. Chrissy is fourteen, Patty seventeen and Abby nineteen. Phew!

I noticed that my beautiful girl was staring at her reflection in the mirror wearing a tank top and shorts, and was softly crying. I couldn't help but walk in to see what the matter was.

'What's wrong Chrissy?' I asked, a hint of concern in my voice.

'I hate my belly. Look at this roll of fat' she said as she attempted to amass a small amount of her stomach into her hand. She was a young girl of medium build so there was no fat in sight, unless she scrunched it up like that, in an attempt to find some. 'And look at these red marks behind my knees,' she said as a tear rolled down her face. I did notice the stretch marks that she was pointing to. In my mind, they were merely signs of growing up. A point she was aware of but didn't want to acknowledge. I didn't find it wise at the time, to state the obvious. That is not what my girl needed in the moment. It broke my heart that my little girl was so critical of the way she looked, when she was in fact lovely. I was not just saying that because she was my daughter. All three girls had their father's height, Chrissy had my straight brown hair and my body type. I was blessed with a quick metabolism, which made it easy to eat whatever I wanted and still not pile on the pounds. That didn't make me or her eat mindlessly, but we could if we wanted to.

In that moment all I did was hug her. The time would come when I would sit her down to have a little talk, about her changing body and what she should and should not focus on. Teenagers can sense a speech coming from a mile away. I didn't want to be that parent. I was the listening and empathising parent today. It wouldn't matter to her what I thought of her body when she was criticising it. You have to know the kind of parent you need to be in different circumstances, with your children.

Why is my mirror not my friend? Discovering True Beauty

You, as a young teenager, often look in the mirror and feel like you just don't fit – amongst your friends, at school or university or even at a family event. You look at your zits, pimples, cellulite, fat rolls, stretch marks, too small this and too big that, flaky hair, oily skin, acne, too much this and too less that etc.

You fail to see your beautiful eyes, your hair, your lips, your neck, your height, your graceful hands, your athletic limbs and so much more. There's a wonderful personality hiding underneath all of it too, and that is often disregarded.

When the timer turns thirteen o clock you start to, as if on cue, feel unwelcome in your own skin. You aim for perfection when that is hardly attainable by anyone on this planet. There is no such thing. Ask all the models in the world and they can still look in the mirror and pick out flaws with just one look in the mirror – yes, the very same people that regular people like us, look at and envy. Comparing yourself to others is a recipe for disaster. Your body and its needs are unique to you. You won't get the answers your body is looking for, if you are using another's body as a reference point. Even a porcelain doll that looks 'ooh so perfect' may have a chip here or there.

One study reports, that at age thirteen, 53% of American girls are "unhappy with their bodies." This grows to a whopping 78% by the time girls reach seventeen. That honestly saddens me. You wonderful young women who have so much to celebrate – your youth, your health, your potential. And yet you feel sad and depressed. I feel for you and I hope I can be of some help.

That elusive self-esteem can be so hard to attain. Feeling confident in your body is a real struggle. You can buy the best dresses and use the finest makeup but it doesn't disguise the way you feel about yourself, when you look in the mirror critically and see that person looking back at you. If you are not comfortable in your own skin, then the rest is just window dressing.

Your body is not just an image which is why I do not like calling it body image. Your body is a canvas of experience that has the marks, scars and war wounds of a life lived thus far. It is a testament to your health and wellbeing or an indicator to something that needs to be addressed – perhaps an illness. Let your idea of your body image not muddy the waters of your life experiences. It's about shifting focus from the physical form of your body and living life in the moment. But doing that or thinking positively isn't child's play or else everyone would do it.

I am not going to preach to you about the positive effects of chanting affirmations. Simply stating them without an unshakeable belief in the deepest part of your neurons about their truth, is not going to be very effective. Telling you to love your body on the other hand, almost sounds narcissistic, doesn't it?

Let's get down to business: Mastering your Appearance and Attitude

Here's what you can do instead. Ponder on these questions. Merely read them and go with the first response that comes up. That is your truth.

- What are the ways by which your body serves you?
- What are the things you like about yourself? (Even if it is just that little mole on your left cheek, that's fine)
- What are the things you don't like but can accept, knowing that it cannot be changed and are a part of you?
- What are the things that others envy about you, that you know of?
- Who loves you the most in the world and what do they say about you? (It can be physical traits or personality traits)
- How does it feel looking at yourself through their lens?

The teen years is all about rebellion. It's about finding your place in the world and being heard and seen. But if you got to rebel, then be rebellious about looking at your body positively, despite what the world and your inner critic feeds you. There is so much beyond your physical appearance. Consider these questions to go deeper – beyond the skin and into the realm of what lies beneath.

- What talents and skills lie within you that are unexplored?
- What are your dreams?
- If you had nothing to fear, what would you do?

If you still feel concerned, speak to an adult or someone who cares and loves you, about your concerns, if you are unable to move past them. Someone else's perspective can definitely help you look at the issue from a whole other angle. Sometimes you might be harsher to yourself than needed.

Taking the reins into your own hands: Empowerment and Self Discovery

It is time to reclaim your body for all that it is, rather than what it is not. It is time to leave judgements and criticism in the rear-view mirror, where they belong.

When it is fixed in the mind, it will be fixed in the body. Look past your so-called flaws and move past the obsession of looking in the mirror for what isn't there. Embrace the good with the bad. Achieve that delicate balance.

Heal your relationship with your body by taking the steps I recommend. So that when you look in the mirror you don't body shame yourself but be more compassionate instead.

There is a whole lot more that you can do to enjoy living inside your body, and that will be covered within the pages of this book, but this first chapter is about just looking at your reflection and liking/accepting what you see. That's the first step, everything else will follow.

Chrissy eventually learned to look at her reflection and smile at the girl who looked back at her. She now considers herself Flawsome. It took work but she got there and you will too.

Yes, your body undergoes changes as you advance into your teen years and how. If you are curious about it, we have got this covered in the chapter that follows.

Summary

- When you look in the mirror and fail to see your positive attributes, focussing instead on everything that is wrong with your physical appearance, it will cause you distress.
- Models and the people you admire have their own insecurities.
- The world can give you conflicting messages that can further confuse you.
- The real regrets are about a life not lived.
- Affirmations and self-love only work if you subscribe and commit to it completely.
- Your body is NOT an image but an experience.
- You are more than your physical appearance.
- Speak to someone who loves you if you feel out of your depth

Activity

You will make the most of your reading experience if you use the section at the back of this book to write down your thoughts, feelings and answers to questions that arise, as you course through the pages of this book.

You can also choose to make any notes that you would like to remember or reference when you're done with reading. There is a special blank section at the very end especially set aside for this.

Your first activity is to answer the questions asked in this chapter and write them down. Your mind has all the answers. It is only a matter of asking the right questions. Don't overthink it, just dive right in.

- Cysts - When the papules become painful and pus filled
- Nodules – hard and painful bumps

In consultation with a good dermatologist, you can use over the counter acne creams to keep them in check. In extreme cases you may need antibiotics but you need not worry about that yet. My girl, Abby needed only one course of treatment, after which she used a topical cream, when she had a very stubborn bout of acne. For the rest of the time, she just stuck to washing her face with a good oil free face wash and keeping her skin clean.

Oily Skin

While some have oily skin that breaks out into acne, certain others may just experience the downside of oily skin. A topical cream to help dry out the excess oil may be helpful in this case. You can also keep a few skin blotters handy in your bag to dab your nose, forehead, and chin to address that 'shiny skin' problem, that may show up in this case. It's very easy to carry around and use and no one needs to know.

Excess Sweating

Sometimes you may experience excess sweating on the palms of your hand, soles of your feet, under your arms or on your scalp. Even while stationary and without any physical activity, dripping sweat is visible appearing as patches on your clothes. The skin around the areas prone to excess sweat, may turn pale and also be susceptible to peeling.

Use a good quality deodorant to prevent body odour and feel fresh. Take two showers a day to combat excess perspiration. A doctor can also prescribe a medical anti-perspirant if the ones available in the market do not do their thing. Choose to wear natural fibres. Definitely ensure to change your socks every day or you will end up causing your feet to smell when you remove them from your shoes. That is never pleasant for anyone is it? Avoid spicy dishes that may cause you to sweat more. You can also wear adhesive underarm patches that can be easily stuck on the inside seam of your sleeves, to prevent wet patches from forming on the underside of your sleeve.

Warts

Some of you may see small flesh-colored bumps that grow on your fingers – under fingernails and the soles of your feet. This can make you feel isolated from the rest of your friends. If you begin to notice these, talk to a trusted adult so they can provide help for you. Laser could help burn them off instantly or maybe a chemical treatment may be your solution. Sometimes they could grow back too. Remember though that these aren't dangerous and typically go away completely after about two years.

Eczema

This is the formation of patches of dry scaly skin, that has a reddish color. They appear in the knees, ankles, and elbow area. Sometimes you may even notice it on your hands and feet. They may cause itching, swelling and irritation to your skin. They are a product of both genetics and the environment. Despite all this you have got to remember that it isn't contagious so there is no need to stay indoors. You can go about your normal life.

Use a good quality moisturiser. And if that does not help, consult a dermatologist.

Also observe any new skin care products that you introduce to your daily routine, that cause this condition to worsen. Keep your nails short so that you do not damage your skin with excess scratching.

Dandruff

This is a skin condition that causes the skin to dry out resulting in the formation of flakes. As commonly believed, this isn't due to improper hygiene or not washing oneself properly. It is just a skin condition that needs to be attended to. Dandruff may cause the following:

- White flakes on the hair, which then fall onto your clothes
- Itching scalp
- Eczema on skin, hair, ears, nose, and eyebrows
- Rashes on other parts of the skin that may look red

All you need to do is wash your hair more regularly. Remove dandruff flakes by brushing hair frequently with a fine-toothed comb. You might need a prescription if you face extreme cases of this.

Now that we have covered what your skin can do during your teenage years, and also how you can address some of these issues, let's dive into your favourite topic, namely cosmetics. Every girl would love herself some makeup now wouldn't she. If you don't like make-up, that's cool too. To each their own. But a word of caution – if your skin is especially sensitive to any product application, then ensure that you avoid any make up products, unless dermatologically approved. You have to live in your skin for the rest of your life. It is best you respect it and its unique needs.

The Art of Make up: Enhancing your Natural Beauty

If you look past the filters on your phones and on the various apps aimed at making you look perfect, the prime rule to remember is that there is no such thing as flawless skin. I tell my girls that they look beautiful when they wake up in the morning – sun kissed and without a hint of makeup. I want them to celebrate and accept that version of themselves above all else. Make up should only just enhance what you already have. It is not meant to cover, hide, or mask anything.

Neither am I here to act holier than thou and preach to you to refrain from using make-up either. A lot of young girls and women love to use make-up. I do too. As long as you are using these products for the right reasons, then it's ok to indulge in them once in a while. If you don't like make-up and prefer to stay away from it, then that is also A ok. It's your choice. Exercise caution and invest in good quality products so that you don't end up damaging your skin. Speak to a trusted adult when you wish to start using make-up so they can buy you the right products, best suited for your skin type and complexion.

If you use make-up, ensure you invest in a good make-up remover and face wash. Removing your make-up from the skin is very important so that you allow your skin to breathe.

Maximising the Power of your Skin: General Skin Care

Have a shower twice a day to clean your skin of dust and sweat. Use a good quality moisturiser or body lotion to keep your skin soft and supple. Always, always, always, use sunscreen. Not only when you step outdoors but also when indoors. If you swim then make sure to use a waterproof sunscreen. You need to protect your skin from the harmful rays of the sun. Use a body scrub once a week to exfoliate dead skin cells. Do not over use it or it will damage the skin. Take good care of your skin. It's a small amount of time that you set aside but it is rewarding all the same.

Summary

- o You may experience acne, dandruff, excess sweating, warts, or eczema during puberty.
- o All of these conditions are a phase, after which they fade off, except in rare cases.
- o Do not self-medicate but consult an adult or a dermatologist.
- o There is no such thing as flawless skin.
- o Accept the most natural version of yourself first.
- o Use make-up only to enhance your look and never to disguise yourself or to pretend to be someone else.
- o Invest in good quality products.
- o Do not experiment unless you have consulted with a trusted adult.
- o Practise a regular skin care routine.

'Marina, honey. It's cut a bit unevenly and a little shorter than it should have been.'

Hearing that Marina just burst into tears.

'Hang on, I might be able to salvage it and make it even, but I cannot do much else. You will have to wait for it to grow out.' My eyes involuntarily went to the polaroid of the two girls taped to Chrissy's mirror. Marina's long blond hair framing her face with no fringe in sight. Hair is such an important part of the way one looks, I thought to myself.

I trimmed Marina's hair to salvage what little I could. I also sent her mother a text as a heads up asking her to go easy on the distraught child. Teenagers can be so feisty and so easily influenced by the things they consume. Now the poor girl was teased and bullied for days till her hair grew out. I felt bad for her.

After she left Chrissy came to me in the kitchen. 'Mom, I tried to stop her,' she said thinking that maybe she would be in trouble with me.

'That's good to know Chrissy. I'm glad you weren't part of the plan. But now she has to bear the consequences of her decision unfortunately, as I always tell you girls.' That just got me a colossal eye roll as she slowly walked away to her bedroom fearing a speech coming up.

Hair hair everywhere

During puberty, other than the soles of your feet and the palms of your hand, the rest of your body tends to be covered by hair. The thickness and density may vary, from one person to the next though.

A bit of theory: Mastering the Art of Hair Care

I don't want to get too technical but you have two kinds of hair on your body. Vellus hair and terminal hair. Vellus hair is the thin, short, and soft hair that covers most of your body. Its main purpose is to serve as insulation. Eg – the hair found on your arms. Terminal hair on the other hand is longer and thicker. During puberty some Vellus hair turns into Terminal hair. Eg – the hair in your underarms and pubic area. An interesting thing to know here is that you retain more vellus hair than your teenage counterparts of the opposite gender.

In certain cases, you may tend to experience hair growth under your chin or even facial hair such as a moustache.

Hair growth varies from one person to another depending on the secretion of hormones (called androgens) and genetics of course.

Another important point to note is that each strand of hair has its own oil gland called the sebaceous gland. This helps in keeping hair waterproof and makes your hair look shiny. But during puberty when the hair glands go on over drive, your hair can become too shiny, greasy. and oily.

Your hair texture like your skin can also undergo changes. My eldest Abby, had the most beautiful, straight, shiny hair as a child. But eventually it became wavy and a little frizzy. It bore no resemblance to the hair she had as a baby. She sometimes looks at her old pictures wistfully hoping to have it back. But alas that rarely happens, if ever.

Hair Care Regimen: Unlocking your Hair's Potential

Make sure you keep your hair squeaky clean. Depending on how oily it can get, wash your hair either every alternate day or at least three times a week. Do not allow dust and the oil secretions, we spoke of earlier, to linger on your hair.

Use a good quality shampoo and conditioner that addresses the needs of your hair. Add in a serum to your hair care routine, post your shower.

Comb your hair when slightly damp with a wide toothed comb so you don't end up damaging your 'elastic-when-wet' hair strands. Do not use a blow dryer regularly as it could dry out your scalp. When needed, in the event that you have to go out immediately after a shower or you have an event to get to, then it is ok to use one. Make sure you spray on some heat protection serum to protect your hair from being robbed of its natural moisture.

Choose a hairstyle that suits your face and is easy to maintain. At the salon, an over ambitious hair stylist might recommend something very chic but it may need a lot of styling and product, which is a waste of time for a busy teen like you.

There are more products than I can enlist, that are available in the market to address different kind of hair. From straight, curly, wavy, frizzy, too dry, too oily, long, and short there is something for everyone. When you try something new, make sure you buy a small pack to see if it works for your hair, before committing to it fully. Many companies may promise you the moon, but the proof is in the pudding.

Also do not over use products, lest they build up in your hair and block hair follicles. There is that saying about 'too much of a good thing' too.

Keep a hairbrush handy in your school bag to run your hair through, during the day just so you don't look unkempt after a sports practise or time at the gym or an exceptionally windy day.

Tie your hair up in a ponytail or a bun when you need to focus on a task at hand so it does not distract you and take you away from what you need to do. You can also use hairbands to keep hair away from your head.

Avoid colouring your hair as this tends to dry your hair out. Opt instead for streaks if you want to try something new. But remember that typically hair strands are bleached before a new color is added, which is never good news. In the long term it will cause damage to your hair. If you are very tempted, then get clip on streaks that can be fixed effortlessly. When you get bored of them, then all you have to do is just stop using them.

If you feel the need to straighten curly hair or curl up straight hair, there are hair irons and hair curlers available to do that. It is better to go for these temporary options that permanently straightening your hair or perming it. After all the new hair that grows will still be of the original texture and this will only be a temporary fix. You will have to end up sitting at the salon for hours every six months or so, to retain the same texture consistently. Using chemicals in the long term will only damage your hair and make it brittle. It may also result in hair loss.

At the right age and once you have consulted with an adult, you can choose to shave or wax your hair to give you an even skin. That way you can wear sleeveless tops and short skirts without having hairy legs sticking out and making you feel out of place. Shaving hair makes it grow back thicker so if you already have thick hair growth then you are better off going for a waxing appointment at the salon. Your mother or another woman at home may be able to guide you on the best way forward on this.

You may also notice that your eyebrows look a little bushy and you may want to get them shaped to accentuate the features of your face. In consultation with an adult, you can do so at a salon by threading or waxing. Be prepared to feel a bit of pain, akin to tiny ant bites, but you'll be thankful when you have beautifully shaped eyebrows. You also get electric trimmers for eyebrows if you prefer that but you might have thicker hair growth in this case, as compared to eyebrows threaded at a salon.

Something to remember: Tips for Gorgeous and Healthy Hair

Every girl's hair is different. Every girl uses a host of different products depending on what works for their hair and their personal budget. Do not ever compare yourself with your friends or those perfect models out there. No one tumbles out of bed with the perfect hair. Models have stylists who work on their hair for long hours to make it look the way it does. All you can do is take good care of your hair and follow a regular routine to get the best out of your hair.

Summary

- Your hair is of two types – Vellus and Terminal
- Your hair will tend to change in texture during puberty
- Sebaceous glands may secrete oil that will make your hair oilier and greasier
- A proper hair care routine is a must to maintain your hair
- Do not over use products and do not use too many products
- Keep your hair in a style that is easy to maintain
- Opt for waxing or threading only after understanding that it is a routine you have to commit to regularly

Activity

Answer the following questions:

How would you describe your hair?

What changes have you noticed in your hair from the time you were a baby to now?

What is the kind of shampoo and conditioner you will need for your hair?

Will you use any other products for your hair care routine? If yes, enlist them.

Have you done adequate research on hair products?

Do you have a favourite hair stylist? Why do you like him/her?

What is the best thing about your hair?

BOOK 2

YOUR CHANGING BODY

*Empowering your Mind and Body:
Navigating Puberty and Mental Health*

INTRODUCTION

This book is a big deal, girls. It teaches you about something very important that will happen to you as a teen.

You will learn about your periods, what to do, how to handle them, what to expect, as well as an exhaustive list of all the products on the market to help you make your monthly experience a manageable one. There is something for everyone, so fret not.

There is a whole cocktail of emotions you will feel during this phase, brought on by the hormones in your body and the unique dance they do every month. Some of you will experience something called PMS. It's an acronym, but as you read on, you will see what it means and what exactly you can do about it. Don't let anyone make you feel badly about it, that's all I'm saying about it at this point.

When I say changing body, boy do I mean it. There are so many things that happen one after the other, all at once and you will feel like you are up and down and sideways. But if you look around you, everyone is going through it. You aren't the only one and hopefully you take heart in that. You will find your mojo.

The book goes on, to cover a very important, yet often overlooked part of becoming a teenager. Your mental wellness. How your shifting moods and emotions from one day to the next, have a huge bearing on how you turn up in the world. Your feelings are valid and you are allowed to take space in the world....that's the underlying message. Treat yourself with the utmost care, if you feel that the symptoms that are described in that chapter, are the things you are feeling. At least now you know more about them and because of it, you can do something about it. By reading this book, you will also learn to be sensitive to the people around you, as you understand the true depths of mental health.

While we talk about the changes in your body and mind, what you put into your body is equally, if not more important. Your food choices, your lifestyle choices, your fitness choices, all add up to the quality of life you have in the long run. Choose right and do right by you.

Then the books gets very exciting as it talks about something a lot of you like and relate to. SHOPPING. Yes, that's right. It's an exciting time to define your own style quotient and follow or go against current trends. It covers all the essentials of your wardrobe as well as a few special somethings. You'll close the last page of that book smiling like a Cheshire cat.

ovary through the fallopian tubes into the uterus, as if like clockwork. This happy space (uterus) is lined by blood, and tissues in preparation for pregnancy. When you are not pregnant, it is your body's duty, during the course of the next five to seven days, to get rid of the unfertilised egg, blood, and tissue. This is when you have your period. Simple.

Now this sounds at first, like you might have a handle on it all, but you should also be aware that sometimes the body doesn't behave as you would like it to. It isn't a machine after all. There are so many uninvited events, people and situations that stir up a cocktail of emotions within your body, that can influence how your cycle for the month will play out. You may have no control over some of these things and they may tend to cause a domino effect. Don't start to worry now. For the most part you can expect your period every twenty-five to twenty-eight days, from your last one but this is an average figure and varies from woman to woman, and their individual experience in a given month.

How can you handle your periods like a pro?

Understand your body so that you can mark your start dates on a calendar. This gives you a rough idea of when to expect your period every month and be somewhat prepared. This will help you avoid any accidents.

Keep a pouch handy in your bag with hygiene products. That way you have them for yourself when needed or you may also be able to help a fellow friend in need. Girls got to stick together after all.

Hygiene products:

There used to be a time when women used to only have pads as an option to use, during menstruation but now it isn't so any more. You have a host of products to choose from. Try different kinds to figure out what works for you.

Pads – There are two options for you to choose from- with wings and without. They are convenient to use and easy to carry around in a pouch to be used when needed. Ensure that they suit you and do not cause any rashes.

Tampons – These are inserted within the cervix and once you get used to it, it's almost like it isn't there, but you need to monitor it. Figure out your own personal flow rate so that you can calculate how many hours it works for you. You can also combine them with pads to be on the safe side and prevent leakage and staining.

Menstrual cups – If you are a friend of the environment, then this reusable menstrual cup is your best friend. You need to insert this silicon cup shaped object into your cervix, which then becomes the receptacle for collecting menstrual matter. It comes with a small extension at the base of the cup, that you can pinch it to effortlessly pull the cup out. You have to ensure to wash it thoroughly after you pour out its contents into the toilet, after each use. You also have to sterilise it with hot water between cycles to avoid infection. Store it in the pouch it comes in or in a box on its own so as not to contaminate it.

Period underwear – This is another product that is environment friendly, as it is washable and gives you the feeling of wearing a pad. If you are ok with the extra work every month of having to wash them, then you can buy a set of four or five pairs so that you have enough of them to circulate between.

That covers what you can expect during the actual menstruation period but what about the lead up to it?

PMS and PMDD: How to Spot and Address Them

What is PMS?

PMS is an acronym for Premenstrual Syndrome, which literally means the symptoms you experience before your period. It isn't only about feeling cranky in some cases and binge eating in others, there is a whole lot more to PMS. Remember I told you the story of my Patty girl.

PMS refers to the physical, behavioural, and emotional changes a woman experiences before menstruation. It recurs during every cycle and could affect your normal life. It causes an increase in oestrogen and progesterone levels in your body. PMS causes a cluster of symptoms. Not **all** women experience these symptoms and not **all** symptoms are experienced by the women who do.

Some of the **physical symptoms** you may experience are as follows:

- Acne
- Tenderness
- Bloating
- Muscle Aches and joint pain
- Cramps
- Headache
- Hunger
- Swollen hands and feet
- Weight gain

Some of the above-mentioned symptoms may cause you to feel low and upset. In that sense, sometimes the mood swings you feel are more to do with being a secondary effect to the main symptoms you are experiencing, rather than an actual effect of PMS.

In addition to this, the other **emotional symptoms** you may feel are as follows:

- Anxiety
- Insomnia
- Angry outbursts

There are also certain **behavioural symptoms** that show up:

37

- Loss of focus
- Fatigue

With this entire bouquet of symptoms that a woman experiences, certain insensitive people associated with you regularly, can refer to your mood swings as 'PMS'ing'. Yes, they conveniently make it a verb. How smug and ill-informed of them. PMS is not only to do with bad moods as we explained earlier. So, do not allow anyone to trivialise what you are feeling or make you feel badly about it. You need to be aware that PMS can sometimes be even more serious than this.

A more complicated version of PMS is PMDD which you will read about in the section to follow.

PMDD – Premenstrual Dysphoric Disorder

This is an extreme form of PMS where it causes hugely depressive episodes before menstruation every month, as if on cue.

How to spot PMDD and address it

If your symptoms affect your personal life to a large extent and prevent you from doing the things you normally like doing, then speak to a trusted adult about your symptoms so they can help you decide on the next steps. Make an appointment to visit an experienced professional to get a diagnosis and figure out what you can do to alleviate some of the symptoms.

Consider some of these questions to help you decide if you need to seek professional help:

- Do you see a pattern every month?
- What are the symptoms that show up?
- What are some of your triggers?
- How can you avoid them?

- How is PMS affecting your life, if applicable?

Other positive steps you can take are:

- Remain active if you can help it. Exercise or walk for about 30 minutes.
- Avoid caffeine, alcohol, and excess salt intake.
- Eat healthy, taking special care to include calcium in your diet.
- Get enough rest.
- Meditate or listen to soothing music to control stress.

After consulting with your gynaecologist, you may take some over the counter pain relievers when absolutely necessary.

Hair growth

When you reach puberty hair, will start to sprout in new areas of your body. Let's see what's going on with those new strands, that erupt out of unsuspecting follicles on your body. Hair is not uncommon as a concept now is it. You have hair on your arms, head, legs, and a few of you might also have fine hair on your cheeks. These have an important function in your body. They help regulate temperature and protect your skin from germs and other curious creatures that have no business being in there.

But during puberty, hair sprouts up on your cheeks, in your underarms and even your nether regions (also referred to as pubic region). The latter two are coarser in texture.

It is normally advised to not shave hair entirely in your pubic area as it serves as a barrier to the entry of bacteria and germs and prevents infections. But this advice isn't written in stone. You can manage your hair growth as detailed out below.

looking like cottage cheese in those specific areas…only it's on your body. That's cellulite. It is fat residing just below the surface of the skin.

Remember that these body changes are happening to all the young girls around you. It's **normal, normal, normal**. The rate at which it happens may vary. The way it looks on each young girl might be different. Some may not experience it at all.

It isn't easy…this whole 'being a woman' thing. But we have gorgeous bodies and amazing legs so it balances out, me thinks.

You should remember that change is inevitable but growth is optional. Knowing how your body changes is one thing. Accepting those changes and the unique road map of your own body is a whole other thing.

Everything new makes you uncomfortable but once you get the hang of it, you'll sail through.

Your daily care routine: Mastering the Art of Self Care

Taking care of your skin and body should be your top priority at any age in life. But as a teenager, with the changing needs of your body, you must take extra care.

In addition to taking daily showers, moisturising, and maintaining hair growth by shaving or waxing, which we have already covered earlier, there are other things you need to do consistently.

Nail Care: Tips and Tricks for Gorgeous Nails

Cut your nails and keep them at a length that is manageable. If you have long nails shape them, so they look presentable. Ensure you clean under the nails. If you choose to wear nail paint, make sure you add a protective base coat, to protect the cuticles of your nails before applying color. Allow your nails to breathe without nail color for a few weeks, or over time they will turn yellow.

Acrylic nail extensions are all the rage currently as they have some really cool patterns on offer, but it is advised to avoid doing them till much later in life, as the technique consumes a lot of time to have them done. You have to go back to the salon to have them removed as well, so they are a big hassle all around. Abby got them done finally on her eighteenth birthday and while she was happy with them, she complained for days on how inconvenient they were while texting and typing as they are stuck onto your nail. You can choose to clip the length but this it's still a point to consider.

Another option available is gel nails, that uses gel on your existing nail length. The longer the nail the better to accommodate the entire pattern. It cannot be done on short nails. I would still opt for the traditional nail paint as I find it hassle free to use but with so many options on the market, I thought I might as well tell you about it.

Take a salon appointment, once in three months for a pedicure, so that you can take care of your feet. I get it. You are a teenager and may not be able to go to the salon all the time. In that case buy a foot scraper to scrape off dead skin, immediately after a shower. The skin tends to soften and you will be able to get it off easily. Use a foot cream regularly to keep the skin of your feet soft and supple. It's a cost effective way to care for your feet.

Summary

- o The five changes your body undergoes during puberty are menstruation, hair growth, breast enlargement, stretch marks and cellulite.
- o All of these changes are perfectly normal and occur at different ages and at different rates.
- o It is better to be prepared, once menstruation begins, to avoid any 'accidents'.

- It is advisable to visit a healthcare professional if symptoms are severe.
- It is normal to want to manage hair growth and also normal if you do not wish to.
- Stretch marks and cellulite are all part of growing up.
- It isn't easy being a woman but you will sail through, although it seems hard right now.
- Adopt a daily care routine to take care of your skin and body.

Activity

Go to your workbook and respond to the questions asked in this section.

Based on the information provided above for hygiene products, figure out what suits you the best and speak to a trusted adult about getting them for you.

Speak to an adult about the ways by which you would like to manage hair growth. They will have the gift of experience in that area and may be able to guide you in the right way.

CHAPTER 2 - MIND MATTERS

"There is hope even when your brain tells you there isn't – John Green"

In this chapter we will cover:
- An understanding of mental health
- How to monitor your own
- Ways to address mental health

Elsa's Attitude: Mastering your Mental Health

My friend Janine came to me one morning, after the kids had gone to school, weeping bitterly. She explained that she had another huge fight with Elsa her daughter who was Patty's classmate and friend. She continued to vent her frustration about Elsa who was being difficult at home, fighting with her mom, her grandfather and her brother. She sulks around the house and refuses to talk. She has suddenly become very destructive and her grades have also suffered.

She seems to be determined to self-destruct and isn't interested in talking to Janine who used to be her best friend. Patty had tried talking to her at school but Elsa shut her up by being extremely rude, so Patty had told her mother she wasn't going to get involved anymore.

Eventually Elsa broke down one day at school and let her rage get out of control. A teacher was very upset and called for her mother. She was asked to get Elsa out of school. It was then that Elsa agreed to go to therapy. She went every week for six months and sorted through her emotional and mental baggage. Eventually, Janine told me that Elsa

Spotting Mental Health Issues and Taking Control of your Life

Social phobia – Insecure feelings when in a social setting

General Anxiety – Worrying overtly about everyday life

Depression – Persistent feelings of loneliness and sadness.

Diving in

Social phobia shows up as:

Dreading meeting people, fear of being humiliated and embarrassed while among people, feeling anxious before a social event, preferring to stay indoors and away from people, struggling to make friends, shaking and perspiring in the presence of others and feeling nauseous at the thought of meeting people or while being around people.

General anxiety can manifest in the form of:

Incessant worrying, lack of concentration, fatigue, feeling angsty and inability to fall asleep.

Depression can turn up in the form of:

Feeling lonely, rejected, invalidated, guilty or helpless, losing interest in things that used to interest you or even daily activities, feeling restless, being pessimistic, having aches and pains that do not go away and having thoughts of suicide and death and feeling fatigued.

How to Address Mental Health Issues Effectively and Live your Best Life

When you hear the word 'therapy' it still causes a few of us to do a double take. But please know that going to therapy is as normal as going to a doctor for a physical ailment. Just like when you are injured you cannot command your body to heal or force it to heal, in a restricted period of time, mental health also needs to be looked at in the same manner. It takes time to heal and it cannot simply be gotten over by ignoring it and not addressing it.

Speak to someone you trust if you feel depressed and anxious, to the point where it is affecting your regular life. This could be anyone from your parents to your siblings, your aunt/uncle, grandparents to even a school counsellor. Choose someone who will take you seriously and with whom you are comfortable talking to about the matter. It is sensitive and you need to feel like you are in a safe space, above all else.

Search online for information on what you can expect from therapy and what a typical therapy session looks like. If the person you have spoken to, recommends a particular therapist, look them up online to understand what they offer and if that works for you. Read reviews posted by past clients. Most often you may not find many reviews as people do not typically like to admit that they went to a therapist. After all it isn't like going to a restaurant and leaving a food review. But some people are pretty open about seeing a therapist and will leave an honest review that may help you make an informed decision.

Do not compare yourself to other peers at school. Not **everyone** needs therapy and not everyone who goes to therapy **talks about it openly**. If you feel the need for it, then it is important for you to take care of your personal needs above all else.

Even if you are in a place where your family or counsellor is recommending therapy, do not go if you feel forced. You should opt for therapy on your own or else you will not be receptive to a therapist helping you, and the session/s will be ineffective. The choice is yours.

On the flipside if you feel the need for therapy and your parents are advising against it, ask for it more assertively or speak to someone else that you trust. You will know your needs more than anyone else. Sometimes a parent may resist therapy thinking that they have perhaps fallen short of your expectations, that you are seeking help elsewhere. Give them the right reasons you need to see a therapist so that you can get the help that you need, at the right time.

Therapy need not necessarily be so, in the strict sense of the word - where you go to an office and lie down on a couch and speak to a licensed professional popularly called talk therapy. There are different kinds of therapy outside of the traditional talk therapy that may work for you as well. Cognitive Behavioural Therapy, Art Therapy, Holistic Therapy, Hypnosis, NLP and so many more. Choose the one that is right for you so that you can be assured that you are in good hands and have started to address your mental health.

If you go to a therapist but you do not vibe well or do not feel comfortable enough to talk to them, make a choice to see a different one. Do not continue to go to the same one in trying to placate your parents or feel like the reviews were good and feel pressured to continue with them when your gut instinct is telling you otherwise. Go with your gut on this one.

Writing can be cathartic. Now whether that means pen to paper or fingers to keyboard – you decide. But when you get all those words out and see it on a page it gets you out of your mind and on the paper so to say. There is no formal way to do this. You can be as organised or disorganised as you wish in your journaling activity. Once you have written your piece, you may choose to burn it or tear it into little pieces or delete the document. You might also choose to file them away or save it for some reason. Again, the choice is yours. This is a method to express yourself. It's a way to sort through the avalanche of feelings and emotions that are sloshing about in there. Who knows, one day you'll look back on these words you wrote and your older self will smile knowing you did ok and also appreciate the younger you for being brave in navigating through that difficult phase in your life.

I know if a teenager hears the word **meditate**, they will run for the hills but what if all those old monks and wise men were actually right. Why not give it a shot. Before you get out of bed and into the hustle and bustle of everyday life, take a ten to fifteen minutes to just sit with yourself in a quiet room. Play calming instrumental music and just breathe – taking long breaths moves your body into the parasympathetic mode which is a calm state of mind. That is why in a panic situation people generally ask you to 'just breathe'. If that is hard for you to do, or you are unable to focus, then there are plenty of guided meditation videos that are available for you to choose from. The key is to be consistent and do it. Over time you will see that your brain has begun to function better. Due to this regular practise, new neural pathways have been created in your brain now that will only benefit you. These new channels in your brain will help you think more clearly, and make decisions and react more calmly. Give it a dedicated effort before dissing it.

Summary

- o Mental health is as important as physical health.
- o Not everyone needs therapy and not everyone who goes to therapy talks about it.
- o Speak to someone you trust so that they can get you the help you deserve.
- o Do your research before you decide which therapy suits you and which therapist suits your unique needs.
- o Change your therapist if you are not comfortable with the one you are seeing.
- o Mental health is a sensitive issue and needs to be handled by the right person.
- o Keep a tab of your moods over a significant period of time to determine what you need.
- o Also look out for other signs of not feeling like yourself or like you used to feel and get the help you need.
- o Try out the recommendations enlisted above, to get yourself to a better state of mind. Try one or try them in combination to see what works for you.

to have some amount of junk food in the house, if they have eaten healthy for eighty percent of the week. They could be veering off that percentage, as I can barely monitor what they have at school, but I'm doing this on good faith.

If I were to venture a guess, Chrissy was more likely to falter than the other two. She is a big foodie. It's a bigger challenge for me to keep her away from it. Patty is into sports and plays football so while she does take in a little bit of junk food, the calories she burns more than makes up for it. Abby and her boyfriend are into yoga and she can move and bend her body like a rubber band. Sometimes I accompany them to class as I am a big fan of yoga too. But for the most part I have my own routine. I prefer to let the couple be, but they have been nice enough to accommodate me when I have chosen to join them. For the most part my girls are healthy and have a pretty active lifestyle. I have to be a little firmer with Chrissy as she hates to workout and hates sports so I'm on it - on this quest to help her make healthier choices as her sisters have. Motherhood is a lifelong journey. There are no breaks or holidays. Sigh.

Eating Healthy: Tiny Steps to a Better Lifestyle: Change Your Eating Habits and Transform Your Life!

You must have heard of the phrase 'You are what you eat'. If food determines your health, the kind of skin you have and the kind of body you have, then shouldn't you specially curate what you put into your body? Yet we all tend to shovel in so much junk into our bodies. Excessive eating and junk food are the new 'normal'. But it leads to a lifetime (short lived sometimes) of physical ailments (diabetes, heart diseases and so on) and of course obesity in younger generations now more than ever before. I don't mean to sound morbid and worry you as you sift through the pages of this book, but I'm here to give you a reality check.

Eating right is integral to good physical and mental health in the long run. Now, you can choose to go to one extreme of getting into diets, that are prescribed to be 'the next best thing', in an attempt to eat healthy or starve yourself, thinking that maybe that's prudent, but without proper consultation with a nutritionist it can prove to be detrimental. A nutritionist may ask you to run some tests and figure out the best plan for you, keeping the needs of your body in mind.

Unhealthy foods taste so good because they are high on sugar and fat and lack fibre and protein. Chrissy read this bit and nodded appreciatively now that she had the complete answer to her question, and not only my philosophical spiel from the aisle in the supermarket the other day.

It is said that an average teenage girl needs 2 servings of grain, 3 servings of vegetable, 1 serving of meat, two servings of dairy and half a serving of fruit. If all this has to go into your body, then your intake of unhealthy food needs to be halved to make way.

Change your eating habits

A habit gets formed when you do something consistently for sixty-six days. Wow, that's a whole lotta days isn't it. But you definitely gain something by putting in all that effort. No pain, no gain after all.

Tiny Steps to a better lifestyle

Change your environment and make it work for you, instead of against you in your quest to eat healthy. The first thing you can do quite easily is to replace several of the unhealthy options at home, with healthy options. If they are not within arm's reach, you probably may not feel motivated to go out and get it, or at best the energy spent in heading out for junk-food-runs, might reduce your intake altogether. This way you are not battling willpower every day. You cannot eat what you don't have and you nip the problem in the bud. By this we do not mean to neglect buying junk food, but in the wide spectrum of options tempting you on the shelves, find out what your specific trigger foods are and avoid those. Think chips and aerated drinks. You can still stack a few items to indulge in, as a change, on rare occasion. Fill your shelves with health bars, cheese, milk, wholegrain bread, bowls of fruits, fresh vegetables etc. so that there is precious little space for crap food.

Reduce the effort needed in making healthy food. If there are eighty thousand steps to making a healthy meal, chances are less likely you'll do it. Look for simple options – easy to get the ingredients and easy to make. Help make the dishes yourself along with your parents. That way you can decide what gets made available and are more likely to eat it. Examples of healthy options could be salads or smoothies. There are varieties that you can make from the choices in the supermarket and it keeps you full for a longer period of time.

Make good portions of food so that you are not left hungry and deprived. That's when the whole healthy routine will pop right out the window and you'll be reaching for all the bad foods again. You have to be sufficiently full after a meal which provides you energy, to keep ploughing through the rest of the day.

Avoid eating out as much as possible, as the inclination is always to go to a junk food place at the mall, rather than to go to a café or a restaurant. The latter will have healthy options while giving you the pleasure of eating out. If you must, choose the latter.

Physical Activity for a Healthy Body: Working out

What you put in your body is as important as how you maintain your body. The muscles in your body need a workout routine to keep them supple and fit. It is crucial to indulge in physical activity. Now what that is, is totally dependent on you.

Sports and athletics are great options to maintain your fitness levels. It ensures you play regularly and also has the added benefit of working with a team.

For those who aren't a fan of sports, you can opt to cycle, run, or go to a nearby gym. Post covid, home gyms have become all the rage. You can sign up for an online class – Zumba, aerobics, HIIT, cardio, weight training, Pilates, dancing and so many more. When you are signed up with a class, your tendency to attend and do the workout is quite higher. Seeing other teenagers exercise regularly and get into a fitter form, may motivate you to commit more regularly. If you are a self-disciplined teenager, then you also have the option to workout on your own. There are several workout routines available online that you can follow regularly to get into shape. You have to find what works for you. Working with a personal coach if you have the time and the budget is the best way to start so that you understand the kind of workout your body needs. A slightly overweight person may need more cardio to burn away the excess fat, but a very thin person might need more strength conditioning exercises than cardio.

Even if you are a healthy individual, staying fit by going for a run around the block or using a peloton always ensures good stamina and all-round fitness. Muscles tend to atrophy over prolonged periods of stagnation.

A Few Things to Remember: Tips and Tricks for a Healthier You

- Make sure to drink plenty of water in between your workout to stay hydrated.
- Wear appropriate clothing to get yourself into the mood to workout.
- Identify the days you can commit to a workout based on your schedule and then stick to it.
- Start slow and build up towards a routine of twenty to thirty minutes over time. Do not dive right in on day one, to do an extended session. It will lead to muscle injuries.
- Ensure that you do not work out all seven days of the week. Your body needs to rest and recover.
- Do not over exert your body and listen to it, for signs of fatigue, so that you do not injure your body.

- Take a break if your body needs it.
- Working out is not only recommended for weight loss, but for overall fitness which every teenager should aim for.
- Avoid vegetating in front of your screens for long periods of time. Sitting for a long period of time will cause long term harm to your body. If your assignments require that you stay glued to your screens, take breaks and walk around or talk to a family member for a while and then get back to your screen.
- Try walking around within your home when you can – while talking on the phone, or choose to take the stairs instead of the lift, if you live in an apartment complex or maybe get the door, when someone arrives. All this will ensure that you stay active and your body moves.

Shopping Right: Building a Healthy and Sustainable Lifestyle through Mindful Consumerism

Now comes the exciting bit. When you make the trip from being a tween to a teen, your sense of style changes quite drastically. You prefer to choose your own clothes rather than have your mom pick them out. You might have an affinity towards certain colors and cuts. You will at this point want to have your own unique fashion signature and that is totally ok.

Trends come and go and then they come back again. Something your mother wore way back in the day, is considered vintage now.

As a teenager, I know there is aspirational value in looking and feeling beautiful and matching with your peers. Not all of you may have the budget to buy designer labels and expensive clothing but that doesn't mean you cannot dress right to suit your figure and body type.

In your world, not only can you visit physical stores but you have the option to shop online as well - try on clothes and return them if you do not like them. You can read reviews to decide if you like a particular outfit. You can also opt for different colours. Some trendy websites have the option of uploading your picture to see if the outfit suits your body type. None of the luxuries I had in my day but that's a story for another time. So, you girls are very lucky, trust me. Since you have access to online shops and can subscribe to newsletters and mailers, you can be the first to know when there are sales to buy clothes at a steal.

Your best bet is to buy clothes during this time, in advance, for events coming up during the year like Prom, Christmas, a landmark birthday. When the event comes knocking on your door, you may not find the best bargain and might have to settle. Do this if the event is not more than six months away, and you do not tend to fluctuate in weight.

Your wardrobe should have clothes for various purposes – working out, casual, school/college, parties, night out and formal events. Buy clothes that are easy to maintain and are of a good quality. You can indulge in a gown or outfit once in a while but for the most part, it is best to have clothes that are affordable and economical as trends are always changing.

Do not feel compelled to wear something just because your friend has it or because everyone is wearing it. If it doesn't feel right to you, don't buy it. Clothes are meant to create a fashion statement but more importantly they are meant for comfort. Abby told me that at prom this popular girl fashioned her skirt out of a thick plastic see through sheet and wore it on top of a bathing suit to look trendy. However, she spent the better part of the evening wiping the inside of the skirt as it caused her skin to sweat, and made the plastic moist and sticky. What a disaster.

Wear clothes that accentuate your body. Do not wear clothes that highlight your body in a way that isn't flattering. You do not want to be ridiculed only to hide the dress in the deepest recesses of your closet never to be worn again. Make wise fashion choices.

Choose shoes that are comfortable and do not lead to a back injury. Some of the heels available on the market nowadays give me a slipped disc just looking at them. Wear the heel height that is appropriate for you. Buy shoes for your workout, sports, hanging out with friends at casual events and formal. Remember not to spend too much on shopping for shoes as you are a growing teen. One growth spurt and those shoes will feel like a vice. Choose wisely and do not overspend.

Buy jackets and sweaters depending on the kind of weather you live in. No point getting thermal wear if you live in a tropical climate. Buy neutral colors that you can pair with various outfits without the need to buy them in several colors.

In our earlier chapters we have covered the need for the right skin care and make up products. It is best you take someone knowledgeable with you, so you do not get swayed into buying more than you need from an eager beaver saleswoman. All products eventually get consumed and you can always buy a different option the next time around.

Invest in bathing suits if you swim or live near a beach/lake or a water body or if you tend to prefer beach or lake vacations. Based on your body type you can choose monokinis, bikinis, tankinis and so many other options, colors, and patterns.

Buy products for your hair based on research on what is best suited for your hair type based on what we covered in the previous book. Buying a good quality blow dryer helps you get your hair ready in minutes as you zip out the door. You can also invest in a hair curler or a hair iron, if you like to experiment with different looks, once in a while. Also buy hair accessories that suit your hair – scrunchies, clips, pins, hair bands to style your hair in different ways to match the look of the day.

Buy pleasant smelling, good quality perfumes and deodorants which are a closet essential. Believe me. I have three girls of my own.

Buy a nice sling back or back pack and clutch. All needed for various purposes. You can also choose to borrow your mother's purses on occasion, as my kids do you can always own some of your own.

Summary
- You are what you eat so choose wisely

- Eating right is important for both physical and mental health
- Consult a nutritionist so you make the right decisions with food
- A habit gets formed in sixty-six days
- Change your environment to keep you on track with your healthy goals
- Reduce the effort used while making food
- Make good portions so they prevent you from grazing throughout the day
- Avoid eating out if you can help it or make wise choices in where you go to eat
- Your workout routine is as important as your food choices
- You can choose from a wide variety of workout options
- An active lifestyle should be a practise that every teen follows
- Work with a personal coach so you can keep track of how your body is changing and stay consistent
- Staying fit is as important as losing weight
- Take care to not overdo it lest you suffer an injury
- Shop to make your own unique fashion statement and not to ape someone else
- Have clothes, shoes, and accessories. products for various events in your life
- Shop ahead of time to take advantage of sales so you get the best deals
- Choose clothes to highlight the features of your body in the best way possible

Activity
Eat right

Choose one trigger food that you will eliminate from your diet and home.

Make a list of five salads and five smoothies that sound interesting so that you can speak to your parents about it.

Commit to helping them in buying the ingredients and making it.

Working out right

Choose a workout routine that you can commit to.

Write out your experience after one month of doing this.

Shop Right

Make a note of the sales in your area – time of year and dates so that you can feed in an alert on your phone to remind you to shop at that time.

Clean out your closet of clothes you have outgrown or are no longer in style. Make a list of the clothes you need under various categories as explained above.

In a world of people pleasers, it's easier to conform than stand out. Social pressure is in that sense, a form of peer pressure. How do you address it and still mark your unique place on this planet? Do you even want to?

Once you slay these monsters or perhaps as you slay them, comes the big one. How do you become independent? It's easy to fight for freedom and push back on rules and guidelines but there is a lot of responsibility that comes with being independent. You will understand what it entails and prepare yourself for it so that you can start adulting soon, just like the rest of us. Spoiler alert – **it isn't all that it's made out to be.**

Whether it is you who choose to move out of your childhood home or it is your parents dropping hints for you to do so, it is inevitable and a necessary part of everyone's journey. You'll face it all and learn to emerge victorious. All you need to do is take one tiny step at a time.

CHAPTER 1 - PEER PRESSURE

"When you say YES to others make sure you aren't saying NO to yourself"

In this chapter we will cover:

- A deep understanding of peer pressure and its perils
- Bullying and how to address it
- How to make the right friends

Abby and Brielle: Navigating Peer Pressure like a Pro

Abby was always a feisty teen during her early teenage years. She has grown up to be a mature young woman now but for a while, it was a bit touch and go with her. My husband Mark used to lose his cool with her and always said I had the patience of a saint. I had to remind him that we were teenagers once too, and had our own share of challenges and struggles.

Abby got into bad company when she was fourteen. Her best friend Mikayla had moved away to Seattle and Abby found herself feeling distraught and lost. At that vulnerable point in one's life, it is easy to latch onto someone who gives you attention and validation. That was what Brielle was to Abby. A rich spoiled brat who was so entitled I couldn't even begin to explain the depth of it. She felt the world owed her and that's how she was with everyone around her, including us, her so called 'friend's' parents. She treated Abby like a second fiddle getting her to do her assignments and carry her things for her from one class to another. She gave Abby her hand me downs. Her clothes were bought for one season or until she got bored, which was pretty quickly. For Abby, designer labels held a kind of intrigue as she knew that we couldn't afford them. She curtsied and bowed and pandered to Brielle's every wish as at that point in her life she thought Brielle could do no wrong. Pointing it out to her was an exercise in pointlessness. Brielle always invited Abby to her home and seldom came to ours. Our beautiful girl was ashamed of our humble abode and looked distinctly uncomfortable the few times her new friend did come around. No amount of explaining and giving her a fresh perspective helped.

They were tight and there was no separating them. The apple does not fall far from the tree of course. Brielle's mother made my skin crawl. She was a saccharine sweet woman who was superficial and someone I wanted to keep at bay. Since the girls were friends that was hardly possible. I suffered that sapping friendship for two whole years. Abby became a version of herself that I couldn't recognise. We were worried when her grades began to fall and, on some days, she distinctly smelled of smoke. A random search in her belongings never yielded any cigarettes and she always denied it claiming someone next to her was smoking. We were starting to get very concerned. The situation kind of took care of itself eventually as Brielle moved onto someone else, after having exploited Abby as much as she could. She was bored of our daughter and discarded her like she did last season's clothes.

Abby was very hurt by what Brielle had done, but this distance made her see what we had been pointing out to her all along. After Brielle's departure, she started to make little changes to her life and eventually made new and better friends. Eventually Brielle did come around to reignite her friendship with Abby but by then my girl had wizened up and told her to stay the hell away from her. It was a little late in the day for her to define boundaries but better late than never, I guess. If there was one thing that friendship taught her, it was to understand what personality traits she needed to keep at arm's length or avoid altogether. She is now friends with a lovely girl called Rebekka. Incidentally it is Rebekka's brother Michael whom Abby is dating and all is well in our world again.

What is Peer Pressure? Understanding its Forms and Effects

As the words say, it literally means feeling the pressure to do certain things, when your peers around you are doing it. It refers to the influence your friends, classmates, and other teenagers around you, have over the way you think and act.

Sometimes it may be little things - dressing like someone else or buying a book that your friend bought which are often the positive effects of peer pressure. But sometimes it's more extreme like alcohol, drugs, and vandalism which are obviously the negative effects of the same thing.

When you are little, (read early years and your tweens), you worship your parents or grandparents and want to be around them all the time, but as you become a teenager suddenly the lure of your friends becomes so much that you spend lesser time with your own parents. You want to be cool, dress cool and sound cool. You want to spend time with people your own age. Sometimes there may be someone in your circle or class or school, that you look up to and envy.

Wanting to be independent and make your own decisions is not a bad thing. It prepares you for 'adulting' which isn't as exciting as kids and teenagers seem to think it is. With being an adult come responsibilities, work, and bills - as if on clockwork. A word of advice – don't be in too big of a hurry to grow up. It ain't all that pretty.

Anyway, back to wanting and craving autonomy. It's a good thing if you make mature, well thought out decisions. But with hormones raging, your friends beckoning you, different value systems of the people around you, the temptation is always to live a little bit on the edge or try something risky or perhaps even wild. But that seldom ends well, although it first it may seem thrilling and ooh so tempting.

Leaning on your friends for emotional and mental support is a good thing because it means you have people in your life that are of the same age as you, who understand you and are there for you. Often times your parents are ostracised from your life, in your bid to hang out with your friends and you hurry to confess your deepest darkest secrets to your friends hoping for a bond to be formed. Your every effort goes towards fitting in, by hook or by crook. But you have got to remember that every teenager comes with their own set of problems, their own unique family systems, and challenges. The question you need to ask yourself is – Are they equipped enough mentally and emotionally to listen to you and advise you in the right way? OR are they doing you more harm than good? After all, they may be trying to fit in and may tell you exactly what you want to hear, rather than what is right for you.

Peer pressure is almost like a rite of passage. It's an unavoidable part of growing up and you experience it in different forms and ways.

Kinds of Peer Pressure

Direct Peer Pressure

This is when your peer directly influences how you do certain things or how you behave. This form of peer pressure is more direct as the title suggests, and makes you take spontaneous poorly thought-out decisions without weighing the pros and cons enough. *Example – when someone offers you a bottle of alcohol or a cigarette, you immediately take it without thinking of the consequences.*

Indirect Peer Pressure

Pressure that is implied. It forces you to mimic another teenager or blindly follow along. It is a more covert form of pressure that is normally not very obvious. It can prey on a naïve teenager, coaxing them to do things they normally would not. There isn't any direct connotation here. It's unspoken. *Example - when you realise that you will only get invited to a house party if you do drugs or consume alcohol you immediately conform.*

Compliance to either of these forms of pressure is a sign of a teenager seeking approval or validation from people they envy and admire. But this can take a darker turn quickly if you are not careful. Wherein you could be bullied for not complying and that can cause long term harm – mentally and emotionally which is harder to recover from. If you remember, we covered this in the chapter on mental health. More on bullying later on in the chapter.

There can be positive peer pressure too, like we mentioned earlier. When you join a swim class because you see another determined teenager take to it. You join a club where you find teenagers that have your kind of vibe, but this type of peer pressure is very rare. I'd hardly like to call this peer 'pressure'. If I had my way, I'd call it 'peer influence'.

It is obvious that both direct and indirection forms of peer pressure, that makes you do untoward things are bad for you. Unfortunately, it is all around you, but in the midst of it, how can you keep your head above water and resist it?

How to Nip Peer Pressure in the Bud and Stay True to Yourself

At your age, it is very important to move out of the mode of people pleasing and into the mode of firmly being able to say NO. If you feel forced into a decision or are distinctly uncomfortable to do something its ok to say NO. It isn't easy to do it, I get that. Even as an adult I find it challenging sometimes, but one thing I can tell you is that my life is way better when I say NO to someone when I am not comfortable doing something, than when I put them first and just feebly say yes. Saying your first NO is truly liberating. Try it!

Understand that everyone has experienced peer pressure in some form or another in their life, including your parents. If you reach out to them and talk to them frankly about the feelings you are going through, they may tell you about their personal experience in being a teenager, and that might help you learn how to handle things better.

Define better boundaries for yourself. If someone oversteps and does not respect your personal space then you need to take a good look at this person, to figure out whether you need to put some distance between you and this 'friend'. Look out for yourself first...always.

If you are a fan of the Spider Man series you will recall a famous quote in the movie that says, 'With great power comes great responsibility'. While it is great being a teenager and wanting freedom, it comes with a certain amount of responsibility – to live honestly and true to yourself no matter what.

Try to go out on a limb and make friends at different places – at the club, at your hobby or skill class, near your home as well as, at school. That way you reduce your dependency on one set of friends, therefore making you more confident to set clear boundaries. If you lose one friend out of the many you have, will it matter as much, than if you had just the one friend?

Be open with your parents and tell them about all your friends no matter where you know them from. This way they get a chance to meet with them, get to know them as well as their parents. Sometimes you may be too close to the situation and may be blinded by how nice someone is being. But things may not be what they seem. Your parents may be able to see it from a neutral standpoint and give you their honest opinion. They have your best interests at heart after all.

I'm sure it is obvious to you before I even say it, that risky behaviour like drinking alcohol, smoking, taking drugs and destroying property have long term repercussions on your health and wellbeing. You may roll your eyes at me thinking that everyone around you is doing it, but it is prudent to show good judgement. You have to look out for you, no one else will. When you are of the appropriate age, having a glass of wine on rare occasions may not be harmful if you have it in responsible company and you do not go overboard. I am not advocating for it but it's one of the things on the list that is ok to do in moderation, at the legal age of course, and not a day sooner.

It's like I tell my girls *'You have to live with the consequences of your decisions'* so make sure your actions reflect what you really want to do rather than because someone else did it or told you to do it.

Bullying: Standing up to your Bullies and Building Resilience

As we mentioned earlier, when peer pressure becomes extreme, you may be the victim of bullying. You might find yourself sometimes in anger, lashing out at someone verbally or someone may hurt you with their words **unintentionally**. Bullying is where someone hurts you **intentionally**. Examples of bullying is when they taunt you in front of others, purposely exclude you from activities or physically harm you.

Bullying also could be where you are forced to do something against your will. But by this point, they may not really request or ask you to do it politely, but force you into doing it. They may rough you up or threaten you with revealing secret information they have about you, which may inevitably force you to go against your better judgement and do it. They may make your life miserable by taunting you or worse stalking you (physically or online).

If all of this starts to interfere with your daily life, where you dread waking up or going to school or you begin to avoid certain places to escape your bully, then you need to address it. The more you put up with it, the more power you give the bully.

Bullies prey on weak people or people whom they think are weak so do not let them win or get away with it. Bullies are people who are typically hurting themselves, due to something possibly going on in their lives or someone bullying them. They just need an outlet to get it all out. But you do not deserve their wrath.

How to handle a bully

Bring up any incident of bullying with a school counsellor, so that they can speak to the concerned person and set them straight in the way that a professional would.

Bring it up with your parents so that they can support you in bringing it up to the authorities. The bullies may be called in and given a fair warning. This might put an end to the act, although a few daredevils may defy the authorities and continue to harass you, in which case you need to make a big noise about it. They should know that you will not tolerate being treated badly. Enough for them to leave you the heck alone.

Whenever possible, save screenshots of online bullying or record physical bullying – voice or video. When you see it coming of course. If you are taken by surprise, you hardly can.

If you and your friends are getting bullied, make a pact with one another to have each one's back in either defending the other , recording the incident, or getting help. If you do not record the incident, then it is your word against theirs. Bullies can be crafty liars. They need to be silenced once and for all. You will be doing someone else a huge favour by talking about it.

Making friends: Tips and Tricks for Meeting New People and Building Strong Relationships

After that unpleasant yet necessary part of the chapter, let's now talk about friends and how to choose the right ones for you. This will make you feel supported, loved, and can hopefully avoid any peer pressure, to be forced to do something you ordinarily wouldn't. The right friends would never pressure you into doing something you aren't comfortable doing after all.

Making friends and sustaining friendships is never easy. It comes with lots of challenges such as peer pressure, misunderstandings, friends moving away disagreements, them not being the way you'd like them to be, moving on to someone else etc. It almost feels like it's easier to just exist alone, but there are far more advantages to having friends than not having them especially if you have the right kind of friends – not the soul sucking one that Abby had. You can have friends who care for you, want to hang out with you, have deep conversations with you, support you, have your back, make you laugh and so much more.

There are findings that have postulated that having friendships makes one live longer, more healthier lives. Loneliness is crippling at any age.

But now for the hard truth.

How do I make new friends?
Be social

It is impossible to find friends if you look at the floor without making eye contact, while out in public, bury yourself in your books, indulge in video games and run home after school/college every day. You must have social skills in order to connect with new people and keep the connection going. Now being social can mean different things to different people. It could mean that you just make an effort to talk to someone at school, or go to a party to meet new people, or a coffee shop or take part in after school activities. This is where you have a potential pool of friends to choose from. The good news about joining an activity or meeting someone in a class you are taking, is that you will have common interests, which is the cornerstone of a good friendship.

Show a genuine interest in them

People can sense fakeness, or when someone comes with an agenda. Take a genuine interest in the person in getting to know them. Ask them questions taking care to avoid being intrusive, but in a bid to understand them. For the most part, people love to talk about themselves, so if they find someone who listens they will be drawn to you. That famous saying – *'People will forget what you said or what you did but will never forget how you made them feel'* is true. Make them feel good in your presence and they will seek you out. Your attempt should be not to have them show interest in you but for you to first be interested in them. When they see your genuineness, they may in turn want to know more about you. It's a win-win.

Do not pick and choose

I know it is tempting to choose the cool kids from your class or people who are just like you, to connect with, but if you are generally friendly and connect with everyone, it becomes easier to have a wider range of friends. Make small talk at a café or the gym or the vet's. A friend can be found anywhere. Imagine losing out on an amazing friendship simply because you didn't start a conversation. Small talk can be hard but with practise it will come easily. Ask a few questions to get the ball rolling or talk about the weather. Keep it going when you see them the next time and before long, you might start to make plans together. Be warned that sometimes people are not in a good head space to reciprocate and you may feel rejected. Look at those as the anomalies, and keep at it. Not everyone will be like that.

Summary

- o Peer pressure is the need to do certain things or be a certain way due to the influence of your friends, classmates, and other teenagers.
- o There is positive and negative pressure, and it is the latter that you need to know how to handle intelligently.
- o There are two kinds of peer pressure – Direct and Indirect. Both are equally harmful and need to be addressed.
- o Your friends influence you in a big way at the cost of excluding your own parents.
- o Your friends may not have the mental fortitude to give you sound advice.
- o Learn to say NO when you mean NO. People pleasing gets you nowhere.
- o Set better boundaries so no one can take advantage of you.
- o Make friends from different walks of life and introduce them to your parents.
- o Avoid risky activities like drinking alcohol, indulging in drugs, and destroying property.
- o An extreme form of peer pressure is bullying.

- o Bullies behave in the way they do because of something that is not right in their own lives.
- o Do not tolerate bullying or internalise it. Speak to an adult about it.
- o You need friends to feel loved and supported.
- o It is important to choose the right friends.
- o You have to make an effort through being social, taking a genuine interest and hanging out at places where you can make friends.

Activity

Bring to your mind and friend circle and write the names of two friends that are a positive influence on your life?

How can you spend more time around them so you enhance the quality of your own life?

Who comes to mind when you think of the word 'sapping' 'draining' 'negative' or 'bully'. Write their name/s down.

What do they do that leaves you feeling drained and anxious?

How can you define better boundaries with this person?

How can you ensure to not let these kinds of people into your life again?

Where else can you make new friends?

What will you do to make that happen?

CHAPTER 2 – MIND YOUR BUSINESS

"People who spend time looking for faults in others should spend time correcting their own"

In this chapter we will cover:
- What societal pressure means
- The downside of seeking validation and people pleasing
- How to become independent and free

A mom was a child too...once upon a time: Achieving Independence

I'm going to go way back in time for this one. Back to the time when I was a young girl of ten. It was 'career day'. We were all sitting in a circle to talk about what we wanted to become when we grew up.

It is important to mention at this time, that I had recently cut my hair. I had shown the hair stylist a short 'pixie girl' look. The kind Demi Moore had in 'Ghost'. But the silly woman interpreted that to be the haircut of 'a military school boy's' or maybe she didn't have the requisite skills. Who knows. After she did her thing, that's who I looked like when I returned to school after summer break. I was already being teased enough but it was the worst on career day. I was a short girl back in the day. One of the shortest in my class. You'll see how this piece of information is also relevant to the story.

Each child had to tell the teacher what they wanted to become when they grew up. Some said doctor, engineer, scientist – the usual. One tall and dusky Indian girl said she wanted to become an air hostess and everyone cheered her on fully believing in her dream at ten. That encouraged me to say 'Model' when my turn came. In my young mind, I was being honest and upfront and thought it would be met with the same hoots of encouragement. Instead, I got laughter and pointing. I felt humiliated and wanted to cry. They all pointed saying 'Model...model...Vogue Model'. They couldn't fathom this petite 'military school boy' becoming a model any time soon. The main source of it was this nasty girl who was the class bully and then immediately, everyone else followed. She eventually didn't amount to anything in her life apparently, the last I heard. My guess is that she was too busy having opinions about other people instead of focussing on her own life. I was upset for days after that, and wanted my hair to grow back in a hurry but that didn't happen. Eventually the ridicule and teasing died down but the hurt and humiliation remained.

Once I grew up, I no longer had any inclination whatsoever to become a model. My interests diversified into something different altogether or maybe it was more to do with the harsh thoughtless comments of my peers. Maybe I shut that option down just as soon as I took it out of the box, for fear of being mocked yet again. When I started to write this chapter, the story just popped into my mind. I decided to tell you about it to help you understand just how deep another's opinion can cut you. We will cover how to rise above it but it also is important for you to not do this to another human being and inflict your negative opinion and views on them either. It does more harm than good – for the most part. But this kind of behaviour may not normally come just from one person from one part of your life. It can come from multiple sources and sometimes even groups of people.

Societal Pressure: Overcoming the Fear of Fitting In

When I say society, it refers to everyone around you. Your friends, your neighbours, relatives, people you interact with at a local club, restaurant, religious gatherings, and parties. Now imagine all of these people having their own world view, experiences and therefore their own opinions.

I know this sounds crass but I read somewhere that *'Opinions are like feet. Everybody's got a couple and they stink'*. True story.

Now whether it's their opinion about your weight, the electives you opt for in school, the kind of friends you hang out with or the clothes you wear. The rule is simple. *'Stop being a busy body and mind your own bee's wax'*. These people who have an opinion about everyone and everything rarely have their own lives in order. It is easier to shine a light on someone else's problems than handle your own sometimes. It is almost like people feel entitled to judge you and force you to conform. There are very few **'Live and let live'** kind of people. Are you perhaps also guilty of this? Something to think about.

People can be unkind in their opinion of you or sometimes too kind, to your own detriment. For example, if someone constantly praises you for how beautiful you look without considering your personality, you may grow up to think there is nothing to you other than your looks. You might have some amazing qualities that get overshadowed by your beauty. It isn't the exterior that matters as much as the interior. I know that sounds like I'm describing a luxury yacht or something but you get what I mean, I hope.

- Who gives people the right to determine your value in the world?
- Who gives them the right to talk about whether you are worthy of being loved and respected?
- Are they there for you when you need to be cheered up?
- Are they there for you when you need a shoulder to cry on?
- Are they truly happy when you win?
- Are they there to help you when you need them?

Yet you unwittingly give them the reins of your life to do with them as they must.

'NO INVOLVEMENT, NO OPINION' is a great motto to follow. This will at best reduce the number of people you allow to affect you in your life and your life's decisions.

On the other hand, there will be people who are very much involved and therefore think it's ok to shove their nose into your business. There is an altogether different approach on how to handle them too, as you will read later on in the chapter.

It is easier said than done to just ignore other people's opinions and perspectives and keep on keeping on. No one is impervious to another's opinion. They can start very early in your life and follow you till the day you die, as morbid as that sounds. The only thing that changes are the people around you who comment on everything in your life, depending on the circles you move around in and the stage of your life you are in.

In order to not stick out or have someone pick on you for being different, you choose to blend in or be invisible. It's a survival mechanism. It may not be in your best interest but you still do it.

After all conformity brings comfort, right? How do you stand out from the crowd when all you get is flak from those around you. Yet history proves that there is true greatness in going against the grain and standing for what you believe in. Not giving two hoots about what other people think. Despite this knowledge, one still tends to conform losing sight of who or what they are because it's easier. Isn't that just sad?

Other people's opinions erodes your confidence and breaks you over time.

Seeking Validation: Learning to Love Yourself and Put Yourself First

Social pressure is a different shade of peer pressure. Doing things because other people want you to do it or because you want to fit in or be accepted. Sometimes you want to feel validated and seek their approval. In order to be worthy of people's approval you have to then be, act and look a certain way. Like you don't have enough on your plate already. *(Insert a massive teenage eye roll here for better effect).*

This monster called 'Seeking validation' is a toxic monster. Some examples of this trait are risking life and limb because you want acceptance - read 'risky activities', responding to someone over a text as soon as you see it for fear of being teased, or being available online all the time to like and comment on someone's post for them to accept you or welcome you into their fold. You want to do anything and everything to please the people around you.

People Pleasing: Tips for Breaking the Cycle and Living your Best Life

So many of us including myself, is guilty of this vice. Why is it so damn hard to say 'No'? Why is it so hard to say 'I don't agree'?

Before you know it, you are neck deep into doing other people's assignments, doing more than your fair share of a school project, covering for someone, or sometimes far worse. These kind of people are the nicest people you'll know but they may not be the most liked. This is because all you achieve out of people pleasing is that you get used by others. You are thought of, when things go south or when there is a problem. You are no one to them but a lifeboat, with no emotions or attachment to you as a person, no matter how hard you try and how much you do for them.

You most often do it to again seek validation and the approval of others even at the cost of your own time and health.

How to put yourself first

Divert your mind – The more energy and focus you give someone, the more they will hound you knowing it is antagonising you and that keeps them going. But if you concentrate on something else that you define as fun, it will divert your mind, even if temporarily. If you like to play the piano or read an especially interesting book, you can shut out all the noise and focus on the activity at hand. Or maybe involve yourself in a sport or anything else that catches your fancy and takes your mind off other people's chatter.

Distance yourself – If other people's opinions are weighing you down and affecting your daily life, then find ways to distance yourself from them. Avoid them or see how you can schedule your day differently so your interactions with these people reduce or can be avoided altogether.

Stand up for yourself – This is probably the hardest of them all. But if you can stand up to someone based on evidence and hard facts, then it's a great way to silence them or deter them from having a go at you in the future. It is more challenging a thing to do but has more long-lasting results.

Reason with yourself – A slightly tamer approach to the same thing is to look at what they are saying logically, analyse whether it is true and if so, is there anything you can do to change it,. If not, is there a way you can live with it despite what these no-gooders are saying about it? Is what they are saying useful to you? – will it for instance fuel you to make changes to your life or are they just wasting time as they do not have anything better to do?

Your experience of yourself should matter above anyone else's experience of you.

When you look in the mirror what do you see?

When you close your eyes at night what do you feel?

When you are sitting on a park bench dreaming what are you thinking?

That's what is important in the end. Focussing on your own opinion. Figuring out how to respect your own self in your eyes. There are people who have conquered that battle and have come out on top. They have become unstoppable. Their way to shut everyone down was by having amazing confidence, being successful and happy. People and their opinions will then recede into the background like wall paper. You start to live your life on your own terms.

The Independent Teenager

'Living life on your own terms'. Sounds exciting doesn't it. But it's something I wish I didn't have to do for so much of my life. It was way simpler back in the day where I didn't have responsibilities and bills to pay.

'You suck' was a term I have heard from my teenagers from time to time. My other friends have heard far worse. Thank God for small mercies. Teenagers are in that phase in their life where they are transitioning from being told what to do to wanting to take all their decisions themselves – sometimes not all great ones. But the fact of the matter as Gary Vaynerchuk puts it is simple – *'Be financially independent from your parents and then you can live life on your own terms. No money, no opinion'*. Or something to that effect. It's a bitter bullet to swallow. Gary is a super successful entrepreneur and motivational speaker who encourages people to work hard, get really good at what they do, and make the big bucks. He gives you a reality check about it not being very easy but it is definitely possible. Unfortunately, you do not have much bargaining power with someone who pays your bills and provides for you. How do you solve this problem and gain more independence?

Set up a bank account

The first step to saving money and managing your investments is to have a bank account. No point in shoving wads of money under your mattress or under clothes. When you see figures in your bank account it gives you a better idea of how much you have and how you want to handle that money. You can take the help of your parents to set up one in a bank of your choice. Nowadays it is super convenient to get things done online, so you no longer have to wait in long queues for trivial things. It saves you heap loads of time and allows you to manage your money at the click of a button.

Find a job

There are so many jobs available for teenagers these days. Based on your schedule, assignments, and skills, figure out what time slots you can carve out to work and make some money. You might see your friends going shopping or to the movies while you are working hard and feel left out. But you need to look at your own priorities. Maybe they are affluent kids who don't need to work or don't care much for independence. If it's important to you then focus on what you need for yourself. When you work, you earn. When you earn, you can buy the things you always wanted and also set aside some for a rainy day. A word of caution to not take on more than you can manage, lest your grades suffer. That will prove detrimental to your overall future. It's also prudent to note that it need not be 'all work and no play'. Make time to hang out with your friends or unwind or else you will eventually experience burn out. Too much of a good thing is bad news.

Creating a budget

Contrary to popular opinion, earning is not only about spending. It is more about saving for the future. It is imperative you create a budget for the month. Look at your expenses and speak to your parents about what you would like to handle for yourself going forward, once you start to earn, you will have their respect, straight off the bat. They will start to see they you are serious about finances and recognise the early signs of independence. Make a list on a spreadsheet of all your expenses – in the present moment and if you choose to move out, so you have the entire picture and can make quick decisions. Make a list of monthly expenses, yearly expenses, and one-time expenses that you forecast are coming.

Once you are aware of what your monthly expenses are, start to create a budget for everything else so that you do not overspend. It is advisable to use the 50/30/20 rule when planning your finances. 50% towards your expenses, 30% towards things you want and 20% saved. The best thing to ensure you save money is to transfer the 20% directly into a different account so that it does not get spent. When you have limited resources, it is easier to stay within budget. Once you have a sizeable amount, you can speak to someone who is good with financial planning to advise you on how to invest it. Money sitting in your account without growing is doing you no good.

Practising Independence

Start the day by making your bed. That's one thing accomplished the first thing in the morning. Make sure you keep your room organised and clean so your parents do not have to pick up after you. Do your laundry and do the dishes when you can. While it is important to do this for yourself there is no harm in lending a helping hand and doing all the dishes or the laundry when you live with your family. It's just good sense to do that. Learn how to do basic plumbing and electrical work to be ready for when you move in to your own place. You cannot be ringing up mom and dad to rescue you every time you run into a problem. The more you know the more independent you become. Learn how to trim plants and mow the lawn. Learn how to vacuum and clean, so your house is organised. All these skills will hold you in good stead for the future whether you choose to live alone or with someone.

Tips for College prep and applications

Have a razor-sharp focus on what you want out of life and how you will get it. You may not have all the answers and you can change your mind. But figuring out what you want to do will serve as a north star. When you know the universities you want to apply to and have a rough idea of the courses you want to take, you can focus your efforts into working hard and getting the right grades to make it happen. Take your college applications seriously, and fill them out as authentically as you can without external help. The college that is considering you wants to know you for you. If you have a diverse range of things you do outside school, like volunteering, a paid job, after school activities, it increases the likelihood of you getting into the university of your choice. It is going to be a lot of hard work but it will be worth it in the end.

Moving Out: Signs you Need to Move out of your Parent's Home and Build your Own Life

What are the reasons you seek to move out of your parent's home?

Is it because all your friends have and you will look like a loser if you do not?

Is it because your friends tease you?

Is it because you want to?

Do you have this fantasy idea of how it will be when you live on your own?

Is it because your college or university is far away from home hence it makes sense to move closer to where you study?

Do you crave freedom and want to have a roaring social life with happening friends?

Whatever your personal reasons make sure they are valid and a good enough reason to want to make the move. Do not feel pushed or compelled to make a decision. You have to follow through once you decide hence it is better to think things all the way through.

Once you have decided do not be in a hurry to move out. Just having a job does not guarantee success or the ability for you to take care of your expenses. Make sure it is a well-paying job and you are consistently working there for a sizeable amount of time before you make the move. When you move, there are already several moving parts and new decisions and circumstances you will be in. If you have a low paying job or an unstable one, you will have to eat humble pie and move back in with your parents even if you don't want to.

You are in an even better position if you are making online income in addition to a regular job. Multiple streams of income at a young age are a sure shot instant ticket to freedom. It's all about the money, at this point. If you can sustain yourself everything else will pretty much fall in place. Online income will also give you a better perspective on whether moving cities or countries is even needed or you can just stay put and still be independent. You can choose to make a move somewhere further along the future when you are well and truly ready. This is not to diss the people who have steady 9 to 5 jobs and where you might be headed. It is just to say that in the present world there are so many more ways to make money than traditional means.

If you are happy where you are – in your parent's home and wondering what the fuss is all about, chances are it may be too early for you to move out. But what are the signs you should be on the lookout for, to decide on what's right for you?

Signs you need to move out of your parent's home
My way or the highway

When you are struggling to be your own person, especially when you are in the latter part of your teen years, you will tend to detest any rules being laid on you. Curfew, chores, screen time, who gets to visit and who you should stay the heck away from etc. Rules are obviously in place so that your parents can ensure that there is some order and discipline in your life. You often hear these statements you *'You are living under my roof'* or *'As long as I pay the bills around here'*. I know this may irk you but you must know that your parents have your best intentions at heart. If they feel defied or that you are perhaps getting into trouble a tad too much, they may be forced to say things like this. Some of you get used to it, you may fight back, push back and sometimes even adhere. But if you start to detest the rules and hate hearing your parents saying these things, then it is time to make the big decision.

Lack of Privacy

When you live in a home that affords you no privacy. For example your room is divided by a curtain or the locks to your door have been removed. Or maybe you share your room with a sibling or a grandparent. You crave for some 'me time'. You have to share your bathroom with someone just when you have found pleasure in spending hours in there with your lotions and potions. You have to share closet space with someone and it all gets a bit too much. If you are organised and the other person tardy that can really cramp your style too. The other way around will bug your roomie as well.

You do not get along with your parents

If your time at home is defined by arguments followed by long bouts of silence and an ensuing cold war, then it you need to decide on what needs to change. Now whether that be something in your own behaviour, attitude or having a talk with your parents or deciding to move out - that is entirely up to you. If you do decide to move, it might actually improve your relationship with your parents. Distance makes the heart grow fonder and all that.

Constant follow ups and micromanaging

With so much happening these days – teenagers going missing, drug abuse, alcohol abuse, bullying etc, it is natural for parents to be concerned about your whereabouts. They love you and want to see you safe. It is agonising to have a child drop off the grid and not respond in an era where they have a phone glued to their palm. I have been on the receiving end of one or two of those, with my girls and it can cause a lot of unnecessary stress. However, if you begin to feel that you are being micromanaged and having to answer for yourself a little too often, then figure out how you want to handle it. Maybe you can text your parents when you reach your destination or pick up their calls, or maybe send them a text if you are unable to. Teenagers who do this do not have quite as much micromanagement. If it still persists and is getting to you then it is time to decide on whether you are ready to move out.

The Neon sign

It may be too early even in your late teens to live independently, but if your parents are dropping hints on and off for you to leave the nest and become independent then maybe it is time for you to take the hint. Maybe your parents have faith in your ability to fend for yourself and feel it is time. It's a compliment if your parents think you are independent enough to go out in the world on your own. It may be a testament to how they brought you up, but also to how well you have adapted and learned to be your own person.

Lack of life skills

Let's hope this isn't the case especially after reading this book. But if it still is, then it's time for you to take the bull by the horns and get down to learning some new skills. It isn't rocket science. You have to learn to keep your home clean, cook, pay your bills on time, order your groceries, tend to your lawns if you live in an independent house and do the laundry, to name a few. Living on your own isn't easy. As a mother and a wife, I still do not have it altogether. You are just beginning, so be patient with yourself. A lot of things you took for granted, your parents did for you. Moving out will ensure that either you have to do it or pay someone to do it. At the start of your professional journey the latter may not be practical and you are left to fend for yourself and take care of it all. Hence life skills are very important, like we mentioned earlier.

Financially stability

If you make your own money, pay a couple of bills at home, and have started to save money then it is a great sign that it's time to move out. Financial management plays a large part in how successfully you are able to run your life. If you have that big chunk of your life under control, everything else pretty much lines up. It's a large part of the pie to get a handle on.

There isn't really a right time or age to move out. Some move out in their late teens, some in their early twenties and some still choose to swallow the bitter pill and live with their parents till they are thirty or even later. Sigh. You got to do what you got to do and what feels right for you. Do not rush to move out because someone else is, but do it for your own freedom and independence and because you feel the time is right.

Once you have taken care of everything explained in this chapter, you will find it easier to make the shift from your parents' home to your own place – a dorm room or an apartment. You will feel better equipped to handle the challenges of living independently. When you are well and ready, speak to your parents about getting your own place and make the move. You are ready to fly into the world with your own wings. The caterpillar has now become a butterfly.

Summary

- o Societal pressure is integral to life. No one is above it.
- o Other people's opinions can shape the course of your own life, if you let it.
- o People's opinions – both positive and negative can influence you.
- o People try to fit in and conform or become invisible in their bid to fit in.

- If the people who have an opinion aren't truly there for you in good times and bad then their opinion should not be considered at all.
- Work on what you think of yourself more than what anyone else thinks.
- The only way out to enjoy an independent life is to obtain life skills and be financially independent.
- Your parents will feel comfortable to have you live on your own if you show them how you will do it.
- Work hard and be consistent in working, earning, and saving your money.
- Learn all that you can around the house so that you are prepared to live life on your own terms when the time is right.
- Don't move out just because everyone else is doing it or you feel pressured.
- Do what is right for you and when it is right for you.
- Look for the signs that it's time to move out and decide accordingly.

Activity

Think of a person whose words have truly affected you in the recent past?

What did they say that bothered you?

How did it make you feel?

Use the suggestions provided in the chapter to think about their opinion from a different perspective?

Did it help change how you feel about it?

If not, what can you do to bring the change?

What skills do you bring to the table?

What places can you possibly work at?

Make a monthly budget.

What universities do you plan to apply to?

What courses do you plan to take?

At what age do you plan to move out?

What do you need to do today to make that happen?

Respond to the other questions in the moving out section as well. They aren't just rhetorical.

BOOK 4

THE SOCIAL FACTOR

Your Authentic Self: Embracing the Power of Identity and Community

INTRODUCTION

If I had one wish, I often wonder if I would have chosen to live in the Gen Z era. It sounds exciting to be able to reach someone immediately at the click of a button, to be able to excuse yourself from a plan without ever having to call or to post pictures of an exciting event in your life for everyone to see.

But when I take a step back, I often realise that I liked the simpler times but that's just me. I bet you cannot imagine a time without cell phones. You must be looking at your parents like they were Neanderthals in their teenage years. But we got by and got by well.

Social media is a great place to be in, but as you nod along another thought also pops up, yes there are downsides to it too. It can be used against someone and can ruin their entire life.

You can look at someone's pictures and not really know if they are happy or sad, healthy, or unwell. Filters you see. Curtains drawn on the realities of life. To portray oneself as one should be, rather than what they really are.

My hope through this book, is for you to separate the wheat from the chaff. To live your life steeped in reality and not be too immersed in the virtual world.

I hope that you aren't excessively influenced by the smokescreen that is social media. Where ephemeral images get likes and comments and you miss out on appreciating the person you are with, or the breath-taking view in front of you. Where you live inside your phone screen, totally out of touch with reality.

It's tempting for everyone...that dopamine rush. But what if you don't need it as much as you think you do? What if the quality of your life improves for the better, by making small tweaks in **how much** content you consume or **how** you consume it?

This book shows you how to look at social media and its impact, the influence it has over you, as **just one** aspect of your life and not your whole life. Make social media work **for you** and not the other way around.

CHAPTER 1 – THE SOCIAL INFLUENCE FACTOR

"You learn the hard way. That's the thing with social media. Nobody knows what they are doing" – Cameron Dallas

The Façade: Shedding the Masks and Finding your True Identity

Stacy, one of the moms at school came up to me one day to chat. Her daughter and my youngest Chrissy, were friends. We spoke about the usual – school, bus routes, the upcoming bake sale, PTA and by the end of it she invited me home. I had my morning free so I accepted and before long was following her to her place. I remember seeing pictures of her lovely home on Chrissy's Insta feed– neat, organised and oh so fancy. I don't care for such things as I feel the personality of someone is so much more important than how their home looks or what they wear. It was a good thing I felt this way because Stacy stopped her car in front of a small house with a neglected front yard, and toys strewn around the dried grass. I contained myself enough to not react to the sight in front of my eyes. I was a little surprised as I recall all of her daughter's posts that depicted an entirely different picture.

There were videos of her splashing in a pool. Lounging on a hammock in the backyard. Taking cookies out of a porcelain cookie jar on a marble countertop. Her beautiful bedroom all done up in lilac. She was clearly in those pictures so whose home was that I wondered as I walked in to see the house in disarray. Nothing was where it should be. It surprised me that Stacy called me home. But she was a lovely woman who was in denial about her situation and permanently optimistic in the midst of chaos. I had my tea and was out of there.

I happened to bring it up with Chrissy later that evening and she just nodded saying 'Oh yeah mum. That's her cousin's place. She goes there once a month and then shoots all her content there to post during the week.'

'Really? But doesn't she pass off that house as her own?'

'Oh yeah Lisa is like that. She told me once and told me not to tell anyone. I think everyone else still thinks it's her place. It doesn't bother me. She is a very nice girl and helps me with my assignments whenever I have a problem,' she said matter-of-factly. *That's my girl*, I thought to myself. *Being grounded in reality and not fazed by what someone has but rather how they are. I beamed a big smile and gave her a hug.*

In this chapter we will cover:

- What False Positivity really means
- What influence the people around you can have over you

False Positivity: Embracing Your True Feelings and Emotions

How many people that you see on social media, are well and truly happy with their lives? All those sun-kissed pictures of women by the beach with their supportive girlfriends, couples entwined around each other, the perfect bikini body and so much more. It is all aimed at making you feel like everyone around you have their lives together while you are floundering like a fish out of water. It is aimed to make you feel bad.

I read a poster in a fancy restroom once. *'We are a sad generation with happy pictures.'* It made me feel so sad. It got me thinking of my time as a teenager. We had none of the pressures that you guys have now. There rarely was a camera in sight during our time out – at a picnic, at a restaurant, at a pub, at a movie. It was all about laughing like hyenas and living in the moment. If somebody did have a camera then they clicked a picture or two. No one cared how they would look when the roll was developed or whether we needed to take fifty more so everyone was happy with the result. We got the pictures printed as is, no photoshop or filters. Yet those pictures are one of my most prized possessions. When I tell any of my girls this story, they look at me like I'm a fossil. They cannot imagine a time like that. Come to think of it, they cannot imagine a time when people coordinated with each other without a cell phone. Patty asks me, 'Mom what did you look at when you got bored or when you felt awkward?' I tell her we just looked around or struck up a conversation with someone. She shrugs as if I speak in an alien tongue. This generation gap I tell you. I wonder what your children will roll their eyes at with you for? Obviously, there will be something that they will not be able to fathom from a generation ago.

Despite everyone's attempts at looking 'fake happy' and posing for pictures that are 'oh so perfect', the reality is that no one actually has perfect lives. The couple who look 'sunshiny flawless' probably had a huge squabble just before the picture was taken. The friends who are posing together might probably be talking behind one another's backs. Certain people are dragged into pictures despite their apparent dislike of posing in them for whatever reason.

It isn't all fake every time but when people want to capture moments of every day on camera, it most likely is. The people who truly enjoy life and each other's company tend to not really want to display it for the world to approve or even want other people to validate their relationship with likes and comments. With that pressure off their backs, they are happier for it. They enjoy life for what it is.

Now for a reality check. You read so much in the news about famous and apparently successful, happy celebrities ending their lives. They leave behind a shocked community, who scroll endlessly through pictures of their perfect families, extremely fun jobs and affluence, things that are enviable and it makes them wonder *'What on earth did they have to complain about'*. You want to make sense of it and you scroll their social media pages looking for a clue past their 'too happy smiles' and their 'I love life' eyes. But there are no answers to be found in those little squares on their social media unfortunately. Because everyone wants to display their lives to be 'more than perfect', lest they get judged by someone else. Everyone feels the pressure to fit in and suffers from FOMO (Fear of missing out).

First it was Facebook but that has slowly receded into the background. For teenagers it is Instagram. TikTok and Snapchat that have their undivided focus. With attention spans reducing by the second, it is all about a quick pic here and a short video there.

Imagine Christina wakes up in the morning, puts on some light make up and falls back into bed clicking a perfectly glowy pic of herself. This gives the world the idea that while they all look like something that crawled out from under a rock, Christina just wakes up looking amazing. Joe sees the picture and wants to feel validated so he puts up a picture of his sneakers talking of how he started a fitness journey just before crawling under the duvet for a long nap. Mindy looks at the picture and feels like she is being left out so puts a picture of her face sprayed with water to say that she had the most amazing workout. You see how this vicious cycle can draw you into a dark abyss. Do you end up feeling good or just hollow? Is it then useful to put those pictures out there when people are appreciating you for things you haven't even done?

Fake pictures is one thing. Then there are filters. Oh, don't even get me started on those. They are added to pictures to make it worth your while, by ironing out those blemishes and making your skin look porcelain smooth. No more pressure to hide that zit. You spend hours editing pictures of both you and your friends, giving the world an idea that your face, body, and lives are just perfect. Isn't that a lot of pressure to put on yourself?

Influence: Navigating the Social World and Finding Your Voice

How often do you want to buy something because someone else has it?

How often do you find yourself looking at yourself in the mirror with disdain comparing your skin, hair, or height with someone else you envy, wanting it earnestly for yourself?

How often do you compare homes, parents, families, lifestyles and so much more?

Where does it all end?

Will you ever be satisfied even if you had all of that?

Someone else's life always seems more desirable and like something you want to have. But like I tell my girls, if you want a part of someone else's life, you have to want all of it. You cannot cherry pick only the parts that you like. Then they scrunch up their faces and retreat into their rooms with nary a word.

You often compare yourself to others on social media not knowing that the perfect faces and bodies you see there, are also photoshopped. Everyone is in the same boat, so you are basically comparing your filtered photos with everyone else's filtered ones. I smell a scam. I don't know about you.

Most people - teenagers included, subscribe to one beauty standard. If you aren't thin and tall then there is something wrong with you? Oh, but why? These standards are so freaking unreal and do not take so many important factors into account. Metabolism, health, genetics to name a few. It's not a one size fits all. It never will be.

But in your quest to look like someone else, you may make an uninformed choice to sacrifice certain foods, certain meals, and experiences and eventually sacrifice your own happiness, coveting something that is a mirage at best.

While the comparison game isn't new, it is starkly different from how it used to be. Before the advent of social media, comparisons were made through the flipping of glossy magazines at a newsstand. What made it more bearable was that those pictures were of models that you didn't personally know. So, you weren't as invested. You could console yourself knowing that they were professional models and there was no way you could look like that, unless you were one too.

But with social media, it hits closer to home. You see 'perfect' pictures of people you know and those that are part of your own social circle which brings the problem a little closer to home. In the early days you could put the magazine back on the shelf and walk away with the image probably receding into the background. However, with your mobile surgically attached to your hand at most times, you are carrying a walking reminder of these images on your phone – to torture yourself by revisiting them repeatedly making you feel worse in a sort of sadistic manner.

When you post a picture, you tend to check your phone over and over again every time there is a new ping. If those efforts are affirmed by positive comments and likes then it creates a feeding funnel to your desire to do it yet again. But at the end of the day, those comments are not directed at the real you but the alternate version of you that you wish you could be. Is that sustainable in the long run?

The time spent editing a picture of you is inversely proportional to how you feel about your own body. Wouldn't you rather spend all that time eating healthy, exercising, and staying fit rather than playing with the photoshop features on your phone to build a false persona?

How to Take Back Control and Be Your Most Authentic Self

I know this sounds scary but stick with me. What if you chose to show the real you on social media if you wanted to be on there, rather than the glossed over 'someone else' version of you? Try posting unedited pictures of yourself. Maybe you will start a revolution and will have others follow suit. After all everyone must be reeling under the pressure.

Write about your experience doing this, on a blog post or speak about it when you get the chance. There will be tons of teenagers who relate. What you do might just help another. Maybe seeing you be your authentic self, may make them do it themselves or perhaps open up to you about it and then slowly it becomes everyone's story but this time the real one.

After all, you need to understand that everyone has bad days. Even the most perfectly coiffed celebrities wake up to pimples, acne and stretch marks. Hiding them does not make them go away but instead it slathers on a varnish of an altered reality. Underneath it all you'll know you're hiding something. It won't feel real in the long run if you keep up the pretence.

If this feels harsh or odd since you still want to face your friends and be seen in public, then balance out filtered pictures with unfiltered ones. Slowly make your way to going totally unfiltered eventually. The only thing you are doing to make the transition easy is phasing them out. It will inadvertently make you compare yourself less to others. Who knows, maybe people will start comparing themselves to you, in how comfortable you are in your own skin?

Summary

- False positivity is a façade that everyone is hiding behind
- All you are doing is comparing your filtered pictures with other people's filtered pictures
- What you see is not always the truth
- You can spend the time used in editing your pictures towards doing more productive thing with your health and body
- Keeping up pretences can be draining
- Make an effort to post unedited pictures of yourself to reduce the pressure on yourself

Activity

Take a couple of unfiltered pictures and decide when you will post them on social media.

What is the best thing that will happen when you do this?

What is the worst that can happen when you do this?

What are the places you can write in or speak at about your experiment?

If you feel hesitant what is holding you back and how can you overcome it?

CHAPTER 2 – FROM SCROLLS TO TROLLS

"We don't really have a choice on whether we DO social media. The question is how well we do it" – Eric Qualman

In this chapter we will cover:

- Social media and its effects – both positive and negative

A Word to the Wise: Navigating the World of Social Media

My three girls and I were sitting at a café. We do this once a month, on the weekends where the four of us gals, much to my husband's delight, go to a café to spend a couple of hours just talking and having fun giving him a day off, from the women's hormonal gravy train. The only rule when we do this, is that we put our phones away in our bags and just be in the present moment. To a teenager that is like a death sentence but it's something I insist on, so the girls have adapted. We have been doing this for several years now.

One Sunday we were at a hearty brunch and were talking a mile a minute when I excused myself to go the lady's room. A teenager was posing in front of the mirror and taking several shots of herself. None of them pleased her and finally she gave up, muttered something to her mother who had just emerged from one of the stalls and walked away without waiting for a response. I was putting on some lip gloss and met the lady's eye.

'Teenagers huh?' she said by way of explanation.

I smiled in response. She came up to me as she washed her hands and continued, 'I noticed you earlier at your table. You have three of your own kids? How on earth do you get them to sit without puckering up for their camera every fifteen seconds?' she asked, her frustration evident.

'Oh, we have a 'no phones' meal or coffee date once a month.' Her eyeballs became the size of saucers.

'For real? And they listen? I can't imagine Sheila agreeing. As a matter of fact, I can't imagine being without my phone either,' she admitted. And therein lay the problem. I had no problem putting my phone away and giving my kids some undivided attention. If I lead by example, then they would have no choice but to follow.

'My daughter is always on the phone taking pictures of herself and posting them. Then she keeps looking at her phone every two seconds to see if there are any notifications. Then she is in a bad mood when no one responds. It's a vicious cycle I tell you. Does that happen to your girls?'

'Sometimes, but not a lot. Not that I'm an expert but I've figured it out along the way. Incidentally, I'm a speaker on topics pertaining to teenagers and have experience in dealing with a lot of teenagers from different races, cultures, and personalities. I work closely with centres that deal with troubled teenagers so it makes my job as a mom slightly easier....I think,' I explained.

'Wow. Talk about meeting the right person at the right time. I'd love to know more about what you do. Any help with that girl, I'd like to take with open arms.'

'Sure,' I said as a fished out my business card. 'My details including my website and contact info are all in there. You can see if there's anything I can do for you. I will be happy to help.'

'Thanks so much Hannah,' she said looking at the card and promptly put it in her bag. 'You will be hearing from me very soon. Have a great lunch. I better get back before Sheila throws a tantrum.' I nodded before she exited the rest room leaving in her wake, a cloud of really strong perfume.

Social Media

Renowned psychologist, Jean Twaney, attributes teenage depression to social media. This stems from her findings that she found a correlation between depression and the time spent on social media. She also found out that teenage girls are more negatively impacted than teenage boys.

97% of teenagers go onto social media every day and 46% are almost constantly on it. It leads to loneliness, feelings of inadequacy, low self-esteem, and high levels of anxiety. Social media is designed to reel you in and keep you on it for hours on end. The challenge is to overcome this 'addiction' and spend a healthy amount of time on it, so that it does not affect your entire life. More on that later.

A critical time for this to impact you even more so, is early adolescence when not only are your brains developing at a swift pace, but your social relationships and sense of identity are also taking shape. Social media affects the way you communicate with the people around you. You tend to send a quick text or a direct message instead of picking up the phone and talking to someone, therefore losing out on an opportunity to connect with that person. Yet, with all this 'over communication', you still tend to be tardy and turn up late, get lost or distracted and oversleep, not finish projects on time and not respond to people. It's all a bit ironical to me.

You tend to strain your eyes staring at the screen first thing in the morning, before your eyes have become accustomed to their waking state. You scroll on a screen in a moving bus. You scroll while you walk, therefore avoiding eye contact or suffer the risk of hurting yourself by knocking into something or tripping over. You are the queen of multitasking checking your phone while you do your homework, study or even shower. While you may be proud of how well you do it all, it will eventually affect your focus and concentration in the long run which is something you do not realise when you live in that young body.

Staring at your screen the whole day prevents you from indulging in physical activity and may cause you to suffer from insomnia. As time goes on, these may lead to more health-related conditions.

Looking at pictures and reading comments online gets you exposed to hate speeches, trolling and racist/sexist comments that will inadvertently affect your mood and demeanour. You may get bullied or may bully other people online, commonly referred to as cyber bullying. It is easier to bully someone online, yet it has more harmful effects than bullying someone in person. When online you can either hide behind the safety of a made-up name and spew hatred or be at the receiving end of this hatred, feeling helpless about how to address it or end it.

Social media affects your brain in more ways than you think. Since it is hard for teenagers to get off their phone, it is almost like an addiction. Not from a substance but from a psychological standpoint. You feel a high when you get validation from someone out there in the world. Your brain releases dopamine which is a feel-good chemical, and in turn craves for more as it involves very little effort.

Social media encourages you to talk about yourself, display yourself and make yourself the centre of the universe. When you have an active audience, it encourages you to do more of it to gain more followers and more engagement. Social media rewards you when you talk about yourself.

If you are one to take pride in your multitasking ability, it isn't all that it is cut out to be. Increased multitasking in the long run reduces your brain's ability to memorise things, once you learn them. Imagine your day being controlled by every ping and ding of your phone. Believe it or not there is a name for it. Phantom Vibration Syndrome. It refers to the feeling you get, that your phone vibrated or buzzed with a notification even as it sits there silently quiet as a church mouse. Your neurological systems are getting wired in all kind of odd ways where sometimes an itch on your foot will make you hallucinate that your phone was vibrating with a notification. It's that weird – this whole dependence on your phones and social media.

But social media can be your friend. You can get something good out of it, if you make the right choices and use it to your advantage. Let's see how that can be made possible.

Using Social Media in the Right Way: Tips and Tricks for Building Your Online Presence and Making a Positive Impact

Post something on social media, then do yourself a favour and post the pic then forget it. Put your phone in a closet or move as far as you can get from it. Do not be teased by its lit-up screen, tempting you to check what other people thought of your brave act or what they felt. Go do something productive like jogging, swimming, reading, or talking to your parents/ grandparents/ siblings. Eventually, you can still see all your notifications but it will be a better use of your time when you see them altogether rather than painstakingly watch each one trickling in.

Curate your feed to follow people and places that motivate you and make your spirits soar. Unfollow people who drain you or make you feel unsure of yourself. If you cannot unfollow someone block their notifications so you decide what shows up in your feed. Make your social media place a happy one. One that you look forward to browsing through rather than feel miserable.

Restrict your time on social media. It is definitely a time suck. Look at it for a set amount of time and be very strict with yourself about moving on and doing something else. You will also have more productive days when you are not left wasting tons of time scrolling mindlessly.

Avoid looking at your phone a half hour before bed. Talk to your family, play with a pet or read or get things organised for the next day. This way you avoid going to bed feeling agitated, upset and are not lying awake for hours on end.

If you feel depressed speak to your parents about it, so they can get you the help you need at the right time.

Make social media about something else. You do not only have to post pictures of you and your friends. If you cook, put up food pictures. If you volunteer at a dog rescue shelter, post pictures of the cute little doggos there. If you like taking scenic pictures, post those instead. There isn't any pressure to show yourself in the 'right way' then is there?

It becomes more about the person behind the face, rather than the face itself. You can post pictures of restaurants that you go to and write reviews and so much more. If you draw or paint post your creative work online, you may have someone who is interested to buy a painting or learn from you, and right there you begin to have an alternate source of income.

I'm just getting started on the myriad possibilities there are out there. You are a smart teenager, I'm sure you'll think of something to make social media a wonderfully enabling place to be in.

Summary

- o Using social media for extended periods of time can lead to depression in teenagers.
- o Social media has so many disadvantages but if used in the right way, it can benefit you as well.
- o Restrict your time on social media.
- o Give this space new meaning by curating what you see and posting pictures of things other than yourself.

Activity

What alternate options can you think of to post on your social media channel?

What kind of content inspires you and makes you happy?

Who will you unfollow today?

What is the time limit you give yourself to scroll social media each day?

BOOK 5

YOUR PERSONAL WORKBOOK

Speak your truth: Discovering your Voice and Unlocking your Potential

INTRODUCTION

Enough reading, more writing in this one. This book is all about you. Your thoughts, your words, feelings, and opinions. It's time to get real and honest.

Journaling has its advantages as you will learn in this book. When I began my research on the benefits of journaling I was blown away. I didn't know there were so many. No wonder my daughter journals regularly. She has all of them locked up in her closet though and only she has access to them. That's a good thing. Her diaries will be honest because she knows no one other than her will read them. Unless she wants someone to.

I almost thought I would skip this section entirely since everyone has access to books and paper and can still do the work. But something about having your journal at the end of the series made it more appealing. I felt there is a higher likelihood you would follow through and write out your responses as there was no need to lug around an extra book.

The questions are very simple and if you respond honestly and with the first answer that comes to mind, you will garner great benefits from it.

There are certain questions that you need to respond to after taking action, and certain things that you will have to commit to and then take action.

The first copies of this book, when published, went to my three girls. They wanted me to sign it like a fancy author and we all laughed about it. I see them reading it sometimes on the porch or sprawled on the sofa. Other times, they are deep in thought, scrawling away in the pages of the workbook, and it makes me smile.

Happy journaling!!!

JOURNAL PROMPTS UNLEASHING THE POWER OF YOUR THOUGHTS AND FEELINGS

I'm glad you made it this far. It means you have either finished reading the entire book or perhaps are done with one chapter and have popped in here to do the activity I have detailed out at the end of that chapter. Either way, I'm glad you are here. Grab a pen and let's begin.

This section is for you to get real. Be as honest as you can be. Make promises to yourself and then keep them. Take massive action. Take charge of your life. And then lock the book somewhere so that no one but you has access to it.

You've got this!

Why is journaling so important? Understanding the Benefits and Power of Self-Reflection

If you have never written your thoughts down, ever before, this might feel a bit odd. You may put it off for days or maybe even altogether. So, read this section if you feel uncertain and think to yourself 'What is even the point of it all?'

It helps you figure out who you are in the truest sense of the word.

It puts a form to your thoughts as they evolve from day to day, week to week and so on.

It helps you find an outlet for your anxiety or stressful thoughts. It also helps deal with your thoughts when you feel depressed or struggle with mental health issues.

It helps you heal.

In today's age when we type on our phones and laptops and everything is digital, there is a certain old-world charm to writing. The more you do it the better your writing style will get.

Writing helps you release any negative emotions like irritation, frustration, anger, rage. It helps you direct all of this into a book rather than at a person and hurting them. It channels your thoughts and helps you make sense of them.

It's your personal sacred space to do as you wish. You can write long paragraphs, draw things, write short words/phrases, color, say things the way that make sense to you. It gives you a sense of freedom in choosing what you want to do with the blank pages and your writing material.

It helps you build a routine if you do it every day. Abby is an avid writer. She has tons and tons of books that she keeps in a locked closet. She tells me it helps keep her sane and that's always a good thing isn't it. It has become such a habit that she takes a book to write in, even when we go on vacation.

You can also begin to understand what patterns keep coming up, what you want to change, what your future could look like, what action steps you need to take to make that happen.

It is the most economical form of self-care. You don't need to spend a lot of money. All you need is a book and a pen or pencil and off you go. It shows that you are invested in yourself and understand the importance of self-love.

You feel relaxed and peaceful after putting all the clutter in your mind on paper. Mercifully, this isn't social media where you will be judged, liked, trolled, or validated. It is just you being you.

Journaling also helps you get creative. It stimulates your right brain and use your sense of self expression. It makes you get unstuck and be in the present moment.

BOOK 1 – BEYOND THE BODY
MIRROR, MIRROR ON THE WALL

What are the ways by which your body serves you?

_____

_____

_____

What are the things you like about yourself? (Even if it is just that little mole on your left cheek, that's fine)

_____

_____

What are the things you don't like but can accept, knowing that it cannot be changed and are a part of you?

_____

_____

What are the things that others envy about you, that you know of?

_____

_____

Who loves you the most in the world and what do they say about you? (It can be physical traits or personality traits)

_____

_____

_____

How does it feel looking at yourself through their lens?

_____

_____

_____

What talents and skills lie within you that are unexplored? Name them or elaborate with details.

_____

_____

_____

What are your dreams?

_____

_____

_____

If you had nothing to fear, what would you do?

_____

_____

_____

SKINTASTIC

Scan your body to see if you find anything that is described in this chapter

- ☐ I did find something that concerns me
- ☐ I didn't find anything out of the ordinary.

If I did describe what it looks like?

_____

_____

_____

Who will you speak to about it? After you do, write down what their advice was.

_____

_____

_____

My personal favourites for my skin care routine:

Body Lotion - _____

Sunscreen - _____

Face moisturiser - _____

HAIR MATTERS

How would you describe your hair?

_____

_____

_____

What changes have you noticed in your hair from the time you were a baby to now?

_____

_____

_____

What is the kind of shampoo and conditioner you will need for your hair?

Shampoo - _____

Conditioner - _____

Will you use any other products for your hair care routine? If yes, enlist them.

_____

_____

Have you done adequate research on hair products?

☐ Yes

☐ No

Do you have a favourite hair stylist? Why do you like him/her?

_____

_____

What is the best thing about your hair?

_____

_____

BOOK 2 – YOUR CHANGING BODY
PHASES OF CHANGE

Do you see a pattern every month?

- ☐ Yes
- ☐ No

What are the symptoms that show up?

_____

_____

What are some of your triggers?

_____

_____

How can you avoid them?

_____

_____

How is PMS affecting your life, if applicable?

_____

_____

_____

_____

MIND MATTERS

What Zone Are You In?

Blue	Green	Yellow	Red
Sick Sad Tired Bored Moving Slowly	Happy Calm Feeling Okay Focused Ready to Learn	Frustrated Worried Silly/Wiggly Excited Loss of Some Control	Mad/Angry Mean Yelling/Hitting Disgusted Out of Control

Date	Day	Mood

NOTE - Fill in the table with a pencil so you can reuse if needed, or you can also make a note of your moods on a piece of paper.

What came up as the prominent mood for the last two weeks?

_____

Repeat as needed. (After an especially rough period, after therapy or whenever you deem fit)

VIVA LA BODY

Eat right

Choose one trigger food that you will eliminate from your diet and home.

_____

Make a list of five salads and five smoothies that sound interesting so that you can speak to your parents about it.

1. _____

2. _____

3. _____

4. _____

5. _____

Working out right

Choose a workout routine that you can commit to.

Write out your experience after one month of doing this. Changes in measurements, feelings, emotions, physical appearance, or anything you notice.

Shop Right

Make a note of the sales in your area – time of year and dates.

1. _____

2. _____

3. _____

I have added an alert on my phone to remind me to shop during the sale.

- ☐ Yes
- ☐ No

Clean out your closet of clothes you have outgrown or are no longer in style. Make a list of the clothes you need under various categories as explained in the chapter.

1. _____

2. _____

3. _____

4. _____

5. _____

6. _____

BOOK 3 – THE WORLD AROUND YOU
PEER PRESSURE

Two friends that are a positive influence in my life. If you have more feel free to add them. You can never have enough genuine friends.

1. _____

2. _____

How can you spend more time around them so you enhance the quality of your own life?

_____

_____

Who comes to mind when you think of the word 'sapping' 'draining' 'negative' or

'bully'. Write their name/s down. If you have more feel free to add them. But you

got to do something about this situation real quick.

1. _____

2. _____

What do they do that leaves you feeling drained and anxious?

_____

_____

How can you define better boundaries with this person?

_____

_____

How can you ensure to not let these kinds of people into your life again?

_____

_____

Where else can you make new friends?

1. _____

2. _____

What will you do to make that happen?

_____

_____

MIND YOUR BUSINESS

When you look in the mirror what do you see?

_____

_____

When you close your eyes at night what do you feel?

_____

_____

When you are sitting on a park bench dreaming, what are you thinking?

_____

_____

Think of a person whose words have truly affected you in the recent past. Write their name down and also what they said to affect you.

_____

What did they say that bothered you?

_____

_____

How did it make you feel? Be as honest and open as you can. This is your personal space.

_____

_____

Use the suggestions provided in the chapter to think about their opinion from a different perspective. Did it help change how you feel about it?

☐ Yes

☐ No

If not, what can you do to bring the change?

_____

What skills do you bring to the table?

1. _____

2. _____

3. _____

What places can you possibly work at?

1. _____

2. _____

Make a monthly budget. These are recurring basic needs and wants. These do not need to cover one-time expenses and purchases. You can make a note of those separately.

Item	Cost

Total	

What universities do you plan to apply to?

1. _____

2. _____

3. _____

What courses do you plan to take?

1. _____

2. _____

3. _____

At what age do you plan to move out?

_____

What do you need to do today to make that happen?

_____

_____

Consider and respond to these questions:

What are the reasons you seek to move out of your parent's home? Tick one or more.

- ☐ Is it because all your friends have and you will look like a loser if you do not?
- ☐ Is it because your friends tease you?
- ☐ Is it because you want to?
- ☐ Do you have this fantasy idea of how it will be when you live on your own?
- ☐ Is it because your college or university is far away from home, hence it makes sense to move closer to where you study?
- ☐ Do you crave freedom and want to have a roaring social life with happening friends?

BOOK 4 – THE SOCIAL FACTOR
THE SOCIAL INFLUENCE FACTOR

Take a couple of unfiltered pictures and decide when you will post them on social media. I took them.

- ☐ Yes (You can even take prints and tack them onto this page as a reminder to your future self on your brave move)
- ☐ No

If you didn't, what is stopping you from taking them?

_____

_____

What is the best thing that will happen when you do this?

_____

_____

What is the worst that can happen when you do this?

_____

_____

What are the places you can write in or speak at, about your experiment?

1. _____

2. _____

3. _____

If you feel hesitant what is holding you back and how can you overcome it?

_____

_____

SCROLLS TO TROLLS

What alternate options/posts can you think of to post on your social media channel?

1. _____

2. _____

3. _____

What kind of content inspires you and makes you happy?

1. _____

2. _____

3. _____

Who will you unfollow today?

1. _____

2. _____

3. _____

What is the time limit you give yourself to scroll social media each day?

_____

AFTER THOUGHTS

What is your personal opinion about this book?

_____

_____

_____

_____

How do you feel after reading it?

_____

_____

How do you feel after writing in the journal prompts?

_____

_____

Who would you recommend this book to?

1. _____

2. _____

MY PERSONAL NOTES

Use this area to write any notes you wish to make at the end of each chapter or as you read a particular chapter. You can also use it to make notes of anything that was like an aha moment or something you wish to remember.

A NOTE FROM THE AUTHOR EMBRACE YOUR INNER SUPERSTAR AND LIVE YOUR BEST LIFE!

Thank you for getting a copy of my book, patiently reading it all the way through, and doing the work. It means a lot to me, especially as a mom to three teenage daughters.

I almost titled this page 'Conclusion'. But it didn't feel right somehow. Here's why. Your journey is just beginning and by the time you reach here, hopefully you will be excited and rearing to go. Even if you are an older teen you still can use aspects of this book to improve your life. Which is why I decided to title it as I have, because I wanted to say something from my heart, just to you.

It's been quite a journey huh!

I remember being a teenager myself eons ago. Despite everything, I think I had it easy. I'm sure my generation will agree. Although I did not know it at the time, I'm glad that I am in a place to be able to write a book like this.

This book was actually conceptualised about four years ago, when I was having coffee with my best friend Samantha. I was telling her about some teenage issue that I was sorting through at the time, and how hard it was dealing with the aftermath of a problem that the said teenager was going through. I told her how sad I was to listen to that your girl and how I wished I could have helped her before the problem became a real problem. That's when she said, 'You should write a book.' Just like that, matter of fact like she truly believed I could add value. And the idea took seed in my head but I kept putting it off for some reason.

But as I continued to see teenagers struggling and battling challenges every day, exacerbated by cell phones and social media, it made me want to take the bull by the horns and help in the best way I possibly could. I finally began to write this book a year ago. I have taken my time but I have no regrets when I see it in its completed form.

My three girls are my biggest critics and have read each chapter in great detail giving me helpful suggestions on how to make it appeal to you, young teen. We have had meetings around our dinner table like a small publishing house. Lol! We have laughed, argued and debated through different parts of the book. They have encouraged the words out of me through pertinent thought-provoking questions and I love them for it. It has allowed my knowledge to flow out in the best way possible.

Mark, my husband picked up the slack at home and school, while I was immersed deeply in the pages of this book. His support helped me in keeping focussed, so I could bring value to you and do right by you.

I hope you enjoyed reading this book, understanding all about being a teenager, and writing out your journal prompts, as much as I enjoyed writing it for you. I wish you all the best in your journey as a teenager no matter where you are on that spectrum now.

Loads of love and luck,

Hannah

Made in the USA
Las Vegas, NV
21 August 2024